People in Vision, Language, and the Mind (P-VLAM 2022)

AA004811

Held at LREC 2022

Marseille, France
20 – 25 June 2022

Editors:

Patrizia Paggio
Albert Gatt
Marc Tanti

ISBN: 978-1-7138-6134-8

Printed from e-media with permission by:

Curran Associates, Inc.
57 Morehouse Lane
Red Hook, NY 12571

CURRAN ASSOCIATES INC.
proceedings
.com

Some format issues inherent in the e-media version may also appear in this print version.

Copyright© (2022) by the Association for Computational Linguistics
All rights reserved.
Copyright for individual papers remains with the authors and are licensed under a Creative Commons 4.0 license, CC-BY-ND. (https://creativecommons.org/licenses/by-nd/4.0/)

Printed with permission by Curran Associates, Inc. (2022)

For permission requests, please contact the Association for Computational Linguistics at the address below.

Association for Computational Linguistics
209 N. Eighth Street
Stroudsburg, Pennsylvania 18360

Phone: 1-570-476-8006
Fax: 1-570-476-0860

acl@aclweb.org

Additional copies of this publication are available from:

Curran Associates, Inc.
57 Morehouse Lane
Red Hook, NY 12571 USA
Phone: 845-758-0400
Fax: 845-758-2633
Email: curran@proceedings.com
Web: www.proceedings.com

LREC 2022 Workshop
Language Resources and Evaluation Conference
20-25 June 2022

People in Vision, Language, and the Mind
P-VLAM

PROCEEDINGS

Editors:
Patrizia Paggio, Albert Gatt, Marc Tanti

Proceedings of the LREC 2022 workshop on People in Vision, Language, and the Mind (P-VLAM 2022)

Edited by:
Patrizia Paggio, Albert Gatt, Marc Tanti

For more information:
European Language Resources Association (ELRA)
9 rue des Cordelières
75013, Paris
France
http://www.elra.info
Email: lrec@elda.org

© European Language Resources Association (ELRA)

These workshop proceedings are licensed under a Creative Commons
Attribution-NonCommercial 4.0 International License

Message from the Program Chairs

This volume documents the proceedings of the second workshop on People in Vision, Language, and the Mind (formerly ONION 2020), held on June 2022 in Marseille, France, as part of the LREC 2022 conference (International Conference on Language Resources and Evaluation). This workshop focuses on how people, their bodies and faces as well as mental states are described in text with associated images, and modelled in computational and cognitive terms. Our goal is to build bridges between researchers from the cognitive science, natural language processing, and vision communities who have an interest in the representation of people. We have accepted six papers this year, three short and three long, with topics varying from automatically generating descriptions of human faces to the ambiguity of emotions to the meaning of nods. We hope that future P-VLAM workshops will continue to have such a variety of topics in this interesting area of research.

Organizers

Patrizia Paggio – University of Copenhagen and University of Malta
Albert Gatt – Utrecht University
Marc Tanti – University of Malta

Program Committee:

Manex Aguirrezabal, CST, University of Copenhagen
Francesca D'Errico, Roma Tre University
Diego Frassinelli, University of Konstanz
Jordi Gonzalez, Universitat Autonoma de Barcelona
David Hogg, University of Leeds
Christer Johansson, University of Bergen
Kristiina Jokinen, National Institute of Advanced Industrial Science and Technology (AIST), Japan
Roman Klinger, University of Stuttgart
Adrian Muscat, University of Malta
Costanza Navarretta, CST, University of Copenhagen
Catherine Pelachaud, Institute for Intelligent Systems and Robotics, UPMC and CNRS
Isabella Poggi, Roma Tre University

Table of Contents

Conference Program

09:00–09:15 ***Welcome***

09:15–10:10 *Keynote - Your face says it all: Automated analysis and synthesis of facial actions*
Itır Önal Ertuğrul

10:10–10:30 *Exploring the GLIDE model for Human Action Effect Prediction*
Fangjun Li, David C. Hogg and Anthony G. Cohn

10:30–11:00 ***Coffee break***

11:00–11:20 *Do Multimodal Emotion Recognition Models Tackle Ambiguity?*
Hélène Tran, Issam Falih, Xavier Goblet and Engelbert Mephu Nguifo

11:20–11:40 *Development of a MultiModal Annotation Framework and Dataset for Deep Video Understanding*
Erika Loc, Keith Curtis, George Awad, Shahzad Rajput and Ian Soboroff

11:40–12:00 *Cognitive States and Types of Nods*
Taiga Mori, Kristiina Jokinen and Yasuharu Den

12:00–12:20 *Examining the Effects of Language-and-Vision Data Augmentation for Generation of Descriptions of Human Faces*
Nikolai Ilinykh, Rafal Černiavski, Eva Elžbieta Sventickaitė, Viktorija Buzaitė and Simon Dobnik

12:20–12:40 *Face2Text revisited: Improved data set and baseline results*
Marc Tanti, Shaun Abdilla, Adrian Muscat, Claudia Borg, Reuben A. Farrugia and Albert Gatt

12:40–13:00 ***Closing***

Proceedings of the workshop on People in Vision, Language, and the Mind @LREC2022 , pages 1–5
Marseille, 20 June 2022
© European Language Resources Association (ELRA), licensed under CC-BY-NC-4.0

Exploring the GLIDE model for Human Action-effect Prediction

Fangjun Li[1], David C. Hogg[1], Anthony G. Cohn[1,2,3,4,5]
[1]School of Computing, University of Leeds, UK
[2]Luzhong Institute of Safety, Qingdao University of Science and Technology, China
[3]College of Electronic and Information Engineering, Tongji University, China
[4]School of Mechanical and Electrical Engineering, Qingdao University of Science and Technology, China
[5]School of Control Science and Engineering, Shandong University, China
{scfli, D.C.Hogg, A.G.Cohn}@leeds.ac.uk

Abstract

We address the following action-effect prediction task. Given an image depicting an initial state of the world and an action expressed in text, predict an image depicting the state of the world following the action. The prediction should have the same scene context as the input image. We explore the use of the recently proposed GLIDE model for performing this task. GLIDE is a generative neural network that can synthesize (inpaint) masked areas of an image, conditioned on a short piece of text. Our idea is to mask-out a region of the input image where the effect of the action is expected to occur. GLIDE is then used to inpaint the masked region conditioned on the required action. In this way, the resulting image has the same background context as the input image, updated to show the effect of the action. We give qualitative results from experiments using the EPIC dataset of ego-centric videos labelled with actions.

Keywords: diffusion, GLIDE, inpainting, action-effect prediction

1. Introduction

The purpose of this study is to investigate the potential of a generative model to reason about human actions occurring in a complex physical environment. The model will be given a textual description for an action and an initial world state depicted in an image; it needs to predict an image depicting the final world state following the action. E.g., given an initial image depicting someone holding a carrot and a knife, and the action 'peel carrot', the model should predict an image in which 'peelings' have been separated from the carrot.

For our action-effect task, the challenge is to generate an output image that both depicts the effect of the action and retains the scene context from the input image. In other words, when peeling the carrot, the kitchen should remain the same before and after.

One way to approach the task would be to treat this as conditional video prediction, extending an input video into the future, as a sequence of new video frames and guided by the provided action. We explore an alternative approach based on a new generative model. GLIDE is a recent neural network model (Nichol et al., 2021) that has two modes of working. In the first, GLIDE generates an image given a piece of text. In the second, GLIDE inpaints a masked region of an image given a piece of text. This second mode can be used to edit images through delineating regions (masked areas) and describing the new content in natural language.

We use the second mode of operation to undertake the action-effect task. In doing this, there are two critical sub-tasks: (1) delineate the region in which we expect the effects of the action to be visible; and (2) express the effects of an action as a short textual description. Typically, action datasets provide annotations for actions expressed only as verb-noun pairs, emphasising the action rather than the effect of the action.

The contributions of our work are as follows:

- Application of the image synthesis model GLIDE to the action-effect task;
- Consideration of how to select masked regions for inpainting;
- Consideration of how to map actions into action-effect textual descriptions;
- Qualitative experiments evaluating the approach on the EPIC dataset.

2. Background on the action-effect prediction task

Human action prediction has been a prevalent topic in recent years, with the goal of predicting forthcoming actions from temporally incomplete action videos. There are two primary research directions: predicting the category of a subsequent action and predicting a motion trajectory. Our action-effect prediction is distinct from both of these and can be regarded as a new kind of action prediction task. Here we give a general formulation of the task.

Given the following:

- An image depicting the initial world state before a human action.
- A linguistic description of the action.

Produce an image depicting the final world state following the action.

For example, in Figure 1, for the action 'crack egg', "the end result is that the entire contents of the egg will be in the bowl, with the yolk unbroken, and that the two halves of the shell are held in the cook's fingers" (Davis, 1998). We expect that given a reference image depicting the action's start state and a text prompt about the action 'crack egg', the generative model can predict a future frame depicting the action's effect, that is, the end world state after the action.

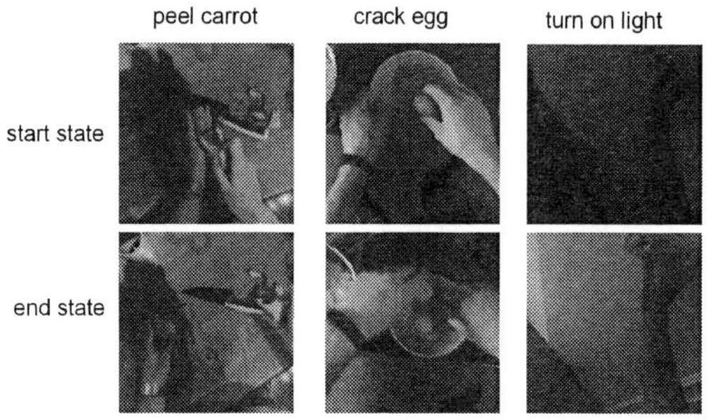

Figure 1: Examples of prediction of the world's future state after an action. The images are taken from the EPIC-Kitchen dataset.

Our task can be viewed as a conditional image prediction problem. Thus it may benefit from architectures designed for image synthesis. Generative Adversarial Networks (GAN) (Goodfellow et al., 2014) have gained great attention since their introduction in 2014. Variational auto-encoders (VAE), which were put forward around the same time, have also increased in popularity over recent years. Recent work on image synthesis using a VAE includes Dall.E (Ramesh et al., 2021). Inspired by simulated annealing and diffusion processes, the use of diffusion models in image synthesis (Ho et al., 2020; Dhariwal and Nichol, 2021) have recently achieved high quality results.

The following logic leads us to focus on the GLIDE model (Nichol et al., 2021). To begin with, we consider generative models that can take both visual and textual input. Following that, we concentrate on diffusion-based methods (Liu et al., 2021) because they have shown superior performance in terms of image sample quality and have well-established model structures that make use of recent advances in transformers and diffusion methods. Finally, we choose GLIDE among diffusion-based models since it is trained on billions of images and can be used to perform image editing (inpainting).

3. Datasets

In general, there are two types of human action video datasets: those taken in the third-person and those taken in the first-person (egocentric).

Third-person videos/images human action Datasets include UCF101, KTH, and UCFsports, Human3.6M, Sports1m, Penn Action and THUMOS-15 (Zhou et al., 2020). These datasets cover human actions like dancing, climbing, walking, etc. The viewpoint is from a third-person standpoint.

First-person (egocentric) video datasets include Extended GTEA Gaze+ (Li et al., 2021) and EPIC-Kitchens-100 (Damen et al., 2020). The majority of the actions in these datasets involve first-person observers holding or manipulating objects. The actions in these two datasets are all about the preparation of meals in a realistic kitchen scenario.

We selected egocentric videos for two reasons:

1. In egocentric videos, most actions are close-ups of hand movements so that the regions of manipulated objects are prominent within the image, which allows for the transmission of sufficient information regarding object state changes after resizing to 64×64 as required for the GLIDE model;
2. The publicly available version of GLIDE ('filtered') was trained on a filtered version of a dataset that excluded all images of humans, so may have poor performance on whole-body state change prediction.

EPIC-Kitchens was utilised as the reference dataset in our experiments because the video quality is better (full HD over 1280×920 and brighter lightening) and the dataset covers 100 hours of recording, more than three times the amount of Extended GTEA Gaze+.

4. Method

The proposed method for action-effect prediction using GLIDE depends on two key elements described in the following sections.

4.1. Setting of Mask Areas

The success in using GLIDE in the action-prediction task depends critically on the choice of the mask region for inpainting. We consider two alternatives: defining a fixed mask and generating a mask tailored to the content of the given image.

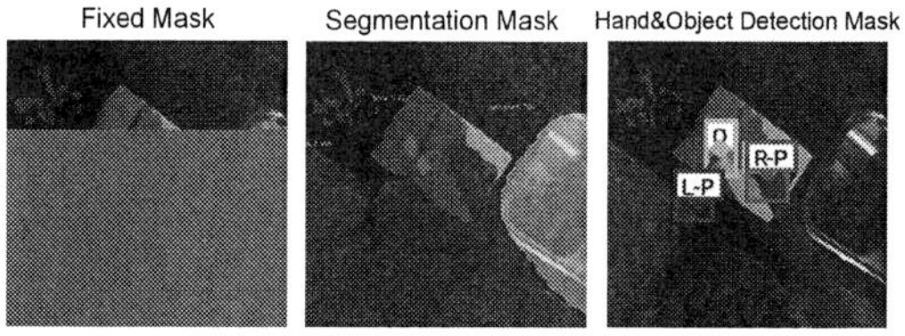

Figure 2: Examples of different mask area settings.

4.1.1. Using a fixed mask

The direct and easiest way to define a masked region for inpainting is to fix the mask area for all input images. For example, as shown in Figure 2 (left), the mask covers the lower two thirds of the image.

The problem with a fixed mask is that the chosen region may not be appropriate for every instance of an action. If the mask region is too big, it may not include sufficient information about the scene context, and the generated image may not resemble the original scene context, except in the area of the fixed portion. If we set the mask region too small, we cannot be certain that the whole state changes occur in that area.

4.1.2. Using a generated mask around a region of interest

For action-effect prediction, the region of interest in an image is the area in which actions are performed. Ideally, we would set the inpainting mask to be this region. The detection of such a region is meaningful because it indicates a zone around the centre of attention, that is where to look for action-relevant items in the scene in order to identify state changes. We adopt two methods for finding masks around regions of interest. In both cases, the regions have already been provided for the EPIC-KITCHENS-100 dataset [1] [2] to delineate the prominent objects within the scene.

In the first method, we define object **segmentation masks** from the regions produced by Mask-RCNN (He et al., 2017).

In the second method, we define **hand and object masks** from detection boxes around the hands and the manipulated objects using a system (Shan et al., 2020) based on Faster-RCNN. In our experiments, we filter the detections to accept only those above a significance threshold of 0.1.

4.2. Generating the text prompt

The inpainted output image from GLIDE is generated in response to a text prompt, which is a description of the effect of an action. We generate this textual description automatically from the action phrase. To do this, we use the pre-trained auto-regressive language model GPT-3 (Brown et al., 2020) to obtain textual descriptions of future world states from action phrases. The input to GPT-3 is a sequence of randomly chosen pairs of action phases with the corresponding textual effect descriptions (two pairs in our experiments), followed by the given action phrase. The continuation of this sequence predicted by GPT-3 provides the textual description we require. We randomly selected the examples from the human collected (Gao et al., 2018) action-effect pairs dataset. For example, for the action 'cut apple', the generated action effect description is 'Apple is cut in half with a knife'.

In experiments, we compare performance with an approach in which the action phrase is input directly to GLIDE as the text prompt.

5. Results

We visually compare performance on the action-effect prediction task with the three mask settings and two ways of generating text prompts.

5.1. Influence of Mask Areas

In Figure 3 we show three different types of action: add, cut, and remove. We set the **fixed mask** to the region that is perceived as the foreground in the majority of action instances. We observe that the GLIDE model with a fixed mask is capable of refilling the masked image with manipulated objects. But the generated object, which is 'chicken' for 'add chicken', 'apple' for 'cut apple' in Figure 3, takes the whole unmasked area. For the **hand and object masks**, the mask incorporates more information about the environment in comparison to the fixed mask. The objects in action can be projected to have a reasonable size and form. However, some vital regions may be cropped owing to the rectangular form of the detection boxes. For the action 'remove lid', the object detection area does not fully cover the lid, but rather the movable section.

With **segmentation masks**, we got better results on these three action instances. For action 'add chicken', apart from the manipulated object (chicken), potato and pot are also masked. The masks are more precise, and there is more visual information: part of hand, the chopping board and kitchen environment, allowing it to refill the pot and chopping board. The resulting picture is more compatible with its environment. For action 'cut apple', the apple is predicted to be of a suitable size and location, but the hand is not created in a sensible way. For action 'remove lid', the pot is well detected compared with using fixed and detection masks. Though the pot shape isn't quite round and the borders aren't perfectly connected, it best describes the lid removed state.

While mask design improves prediction, there is still room for improvement: the model cannot include any information about the manipulated object, thus the newly produced objects are not exactly those that appeared in the start frame.

5.2. Influence of Text Prompts

The effect description for the action "add chicken" as shown in Figure 3 comes from GPT-3. In comparison to a pure action phrase, the text prompt "After add chicken, there are now chicken in the pot." contains more detailed information regarding the effects of an action, specifically that the chicken is now in the pot. We can observe that, with this text prompt, in all predicted images, the chicken is in the pot. We can also observe apparent improvement in generation results with a fixed mask on the action "cut apple" and segmentation mask on action "remove lid". We can see a noticeable improvement in generation image quality on action "cut apple" with fixed mask and action "remove lid" with segmentation mask.

[1] https://github.com/epic-kitchens/epic-kitchens-100-object-masks

[2] https://github.com/epic-kitchens/epic-kitchens-100-hand-object-bboxes

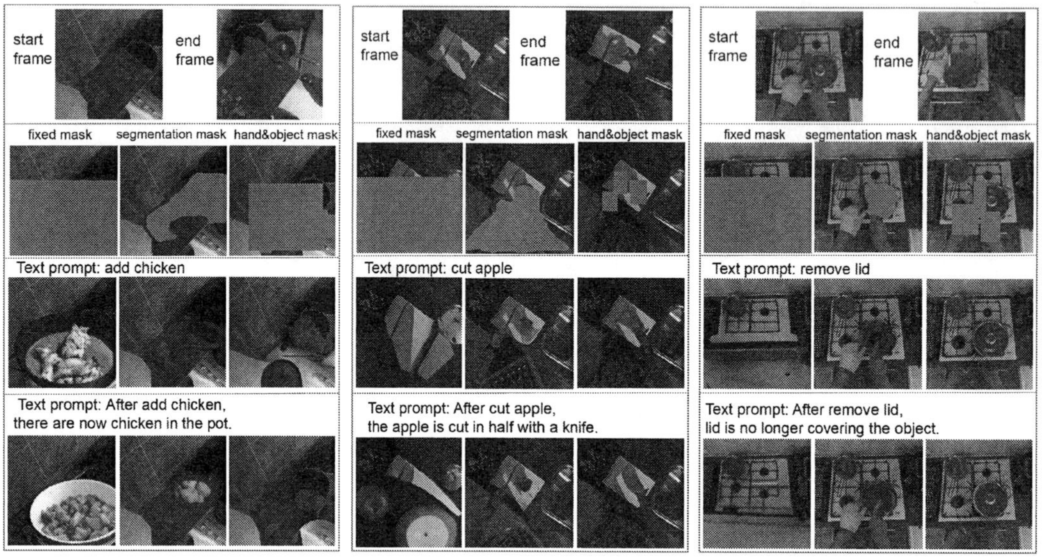

Figure 3: Examples of action-effect prediction on action "add chicken" (left), "cut apple" (middle) and "remove lid" (right) with GLIDE using different masks and text prompts. Within the panel for each action are shown the original start and end frames from the dataset (top row), the three masks (2nd row), the results using the action phrase as the text prompt to GLIDE (3rd row), and the results using the effect description from GPT-3 as the text prompt to GLIDE (4th row)

5.3. Failure cases

In Figure 4 we show several failure cases: some actions that involve changing the brightness of the environment rather than changing the attributes of items, e.g., 'turn on light'; certain position-changing actions such as 'switch cupboard' (i.e. open or close cupboard); and object-quantity-increasing actions such as 'cut carrots' and 'peel garlic', the initial masked area may be insufficiently large to fully fill in the newly formed pieces.

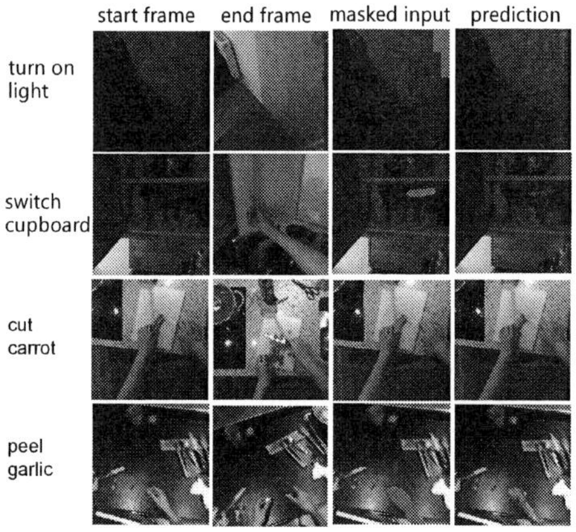

Figure 4: Failure examples using segmentation mask and action phrase as text prompt.

6. Conclusions and Future Work

We have explored GLIDE's potential on our real-world action-effect prediction task. We have shown that by optimising the mask area design and converting actions into action-effect descriptions as text prompts, the GLIDE model can create more accurate predictions that are consistent with the start world state.

In future work, we plan to fine-tune GLIDE for our action-effect task using a specialised dataset. It would also be interesting to explore whether GLIDE could be developed to avoid the use of a mask and instead revise the whole image based on a text prompt.

7. References

Brown, T. B., Mann, B., Ryder, N., Subbiah, M., Kaplan, J., Dhariwal, P., Neelakantan, A., Shyam, P., Sastry, G., Askell, A., et al. (2020). Language models are few-shot learners. *arXiv preprint arXiv:2005.14165*.

Damen, D., Doughty, H., Farinella, G. M., Fidler, S., Furnari, A., Kazakos, E., Moltisanti, D., Munro, J., Perrett, T., Price, W., et al. (2020). The epic-kitchens dataset: Collection, challenges and baselines. *IEEE Transactions on Pattern Analysis and Machine Intelligence*, 43(11):4125–4141.

Davis, E. (1998). Naive physics perplex. *AI magazine*, 19(4):51–51.

Dhariwal, P. and Nichol, A. (2021). Diffusion models

beat gans on image synthesis. *Advances in Neural Information Processing Systems*, 34.

Gao, Q., Yang, S., Chai, J., and Vanderwende, L. (2018). What action causes this? towards naive physical action-effect prediction. In *Proceedings of the 56th Annual Meeting of the Association for Computational Linguistics (Volume 1: Long Papers)*, pages 934–945.

Goodfellow, I., Pouget-Abadie, J., Mirza, M., Xu, B., Warde-Farley, D., Ozair, S., Courville, A., and Bengio, Y. (2014). Generative adversarial nets. *Advances in neural information processing systems*, 27.

He, K., Gkioxari, G., Dollár, P., and Girshick, R. (2017). Mask r-cnn. In *Proceedings of the IEEE international conference on computer vision*, pages 2961–2969.

Ho, J., Jain, A., and Abbeel, P. (2020). Denoising diffusion probabilistic models. *Advances in Neural Information Processing Systems*, 33:6840–6851.

Li, Y., Liu, M., and Rehg, J. (2021). In the eye of the beholder: Gaze and actions in first person video. *IEEE Transactions on Pattern Analysis and Machine Intelligence*.

Liu, X., Park, D. H., Azadi, S., Zhang, G., Chopikyan, A., Hu, Y., Shi, H., Rohrbach, A., and Darrell, T. (2021). More control for free! image synthesis with semantic diffusion guidance. *arXiv preprint arXiv:2112.05744*.

Nichol, A., Dhariwal, P., Ramesh, A., Shyam, P., Mishkin, P., McGrew, B., Sutskever, I., and Chen, M. (2021). Glide: Towards photorealistic image generation and editing with text-guided diffusion models. *arXiv preprint arXiv:2112.10741*.

Ramesh, A., Pavlov, M., Goh, G., Gray, S., Voss, C., Radford, A., Chen, M., and Sutskever, I. (2021). Zero-shot text-to-image generation. In *International Conference on Machine Learning*, pages 8821–8831. PMLR.

Shan, D., Geng, J., Shu, M., and Fouhey, D. F. (2020). Understanding human hands in contact at internet scale. In *Proceedings of the IEEE/CVF conference on computer vision and pattern recognition*, pages 9869–9878.

Zhou, Y., Dong, H., and El Saddik, A. (2020). Deep learning in next-frame prediction: A benchmark review. *IEEE Access*, 8:69273–69283.

Proceedings of the workshop on People in Vision, Language, and the Mind @LREC2022, pages 6–11
Marseille, 20 June 2022
© European Language Resources Association (ELRA), licensed under CC-BY-NC-4.0

Do Multimodal Emotion Recognition Models Tackle Ambiguity?

Hélène Tran[1,2], Issam Falih[1], Xavier Goblet[2], Engelbert Mephu Nguifo[1]
[1]Université Clermont-Auvergne, CNRS, Mines de Saint-Étienne,
Clermont-Auvergne-INP, LIMOS, 63000 Clermont-Ferrand, France
[2]Jeolis Solutions, 63000 Clermont-Ferrand, France
helene.tran@doctorant.uca.fr, {issam.falih, engelbert.mephu_nguifo}@uca.fr
xavier.goblet@lojelis.com

Abstract

Most databases used for emotion recognition assign a single emotion to data samples. This does not match with the complex nature of emotions: we can feel a wide range of emotions throughout our lives with varying degrees of intensity. We may even experience multiple emotions at once. Furthermore, each person physically expresses emotions differently, which makes emotion recognition even more challenging: we call this emotional ambiguity. This paper investigates the problem as a review of ambiguity in multimodal emotion recognition models. To lay the groundwork, the main representations of emotions along with solutions for incorporating ambiguity are described, followed by a brief overview of ambiguity representation in multimodal databases. Thereafter, only models trained on a database that incorporates ambiguity have been studied in this paper. We conclude that although databases provide annotations with ambiguity, most of these models do not fully exploit them, showing that there is still room for improvement in multimodal emotion recognition systems.

Keywords: Multimodal learning, Emotion recognition, Ambiguity

1. Introduction

Emotions have always played a fundamental role in human decision making, from choosing what to eat for lunch to choosing a professional career path. Identifying our emotions, understanding why we are experiencing them, and how to act accordingly are essential to our well-being: this is emotional intelligence. Therefore, support systems for patient education must be able to identify user emotion in order to offer tailored content and maintain user motivation in the long term. Emotion recognition can benefit various other applications such as remote patient follow-up, recommendation systems, and gaming experience.

The development of emotion recognition systems comes with its own challenges. First, many researchers recommend combining multiple sources of information (e.g., voice, text, facial expression) to perform emotion recognition. This is not surprising given the multimodal nature of emotional expression and the human ability to manipulate facial expression or spoken words. Second, the identification, expression, and recognition of emotions can sometimes be tricky, due to the ambiguous nature of emotions. Ambiguity and uncertainty, although closely related, are two distinct ideas: while uncertainty refers to what is not certain to be observed, ambiguity refers to an equivocal trait, where the observed emotion may be confusing. For instance, anger and disgust are two emotions with similar facial expression features. Observing a slightly raised corner of the lip can be open to interpretation (e.g., sarcasm, satisfaction). Emotional ambiguity also includes the observation of several emotions: for example, anger is often mixed with sadness. As a result, databases and machine learning models should consider ambiguity in emotion representation to match what is observed in real life and thus developing more accurate models.

Given the two above challenges, our main objective is to implement a multimodal emotion recognition system based on facial expression, voice, and text data, while taking ambiguity into account. To this end, the paper offers a review of ambiguity in multimodal emotion recognition models by reporting the emotional representation produced in the model output.

The rest of the paper is divided as follows: section 2 presents the two main neural architectures used for model categorisation in the review. Section 3 describes the current emotion representations in the literature and how ambiguity can be incorporated. Section 4 gives a brief overview of multimodal databases that attempt to represent ambiguity, while section 5 is a review of multimodal emotion recognition models with a study of emotion representations in the output. Section 6 discusses their position regarding emotion ambiguity and section 7 concludes the paper with future works.

2. Background

This section describes the main neural architectures involved in the models of our review presented in section 5: recurrent neural networks and transformers.

2.1. Recurrent Neural Networks

Considering the time dimension is relevant when working with sequences. Recurrent neural networks (RNN) are a sub-family of neural architectures designed to operate on temporal sequences. They are equipped with memory cells to save internal states while processing temporal data sequentially. The most popular RNNs are bidirectional, long short-term memory (LSTM) and gated recurrent units (GRU).

Bidirectional RNNs, presented by Schuster and Paliwal (1997), are composed of two hidden layers which read the input sequence in the forward and backward direction respectively. LSTM and GRU networks, introduced by Hochreiter and Schmidhuber (1997) and Cho et al. (2014) respectively, intend to mitigate the vanishing gradient that traditional RNNs regularly face. The vanishing gradient happens during backpropagation when the gradient becomes smaller and smaller as we come close to the earliest timepoints, until there is no weight update; in this case, the effects of earlier inputs are not learned anymore. LSTM and GRU have similar architecture, with fewer parameters for GRU.

2.2. Transformers

Vaswani et al. (2017) presented a groundbreaking network that has quickly become the basis of numerous deep learning models: transformers. This architecture is an encoder-decoder system that transforms one sequence into another. Transformers rely on an attention mechanism: they identify parts of the sequence representing key information and assign them a higher weight. Since they process sequences as a whole, transformers show better performance than RNNs which rely on long-term dependency and thus face the problem of vanishing gradients. Transformers were originally designed to perform translation tasks and are now widely used in natural language processing.

3. Current Emotion Representations

This section gives an overview of the current emotion representations found in the literature. Subsection 3.1 describes the two main emotional models: discrete and continuous. Subsection 3.2 presents the main limitation of current emotional representations while subsection 3.3 depicts approaches to incorporate ambiguity.

3.1. Main Emotion Representations

The two main representations of emotions are:

- **Discrete.** Emotions are represented by discrete affective states. The most popular list of emotions used in affective computing is that of Ekman (1992): anger, disgust, fear, joy, sadness, and surprise. Another common discrete emotional model is the Wheel of Emotions proposed by Plutchik (2001) which comprises of four pairs of opposite emotions (joy and sadness, trust and disgust, fear and anger, anticipation and surprise) with four degrees of intensity for each emotion (figure 1).

- **Continuous.** Emotions are placed in a multidimensional space. The two main dimensions are *valence* (pleasantness) and *arousal* (measure of physiological activity felt). A third dimension can be added such as *dominance* (Russell and Mehrabian, 1977), which refers to one's ability to take action on the situation, or *potency* (Schlosberg, 1954) which estimates the attention or rejection level towards an object, person, or situation.

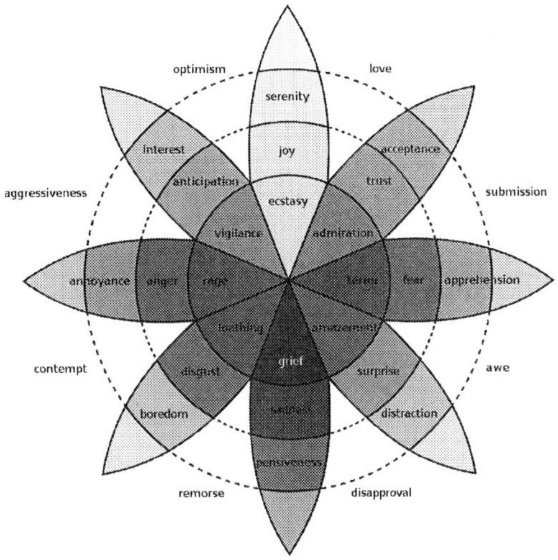

Figure 1: Plutchik's Wheel of Emotions

3.2. Limitation of Current Emotion Representations

Emotions are often represented as a single point. In the discrete approach, only one emotion can be recognized in each sample. In the continuous approach, a single point representing the emotion moves over time in the multidimensional space.

Choosing a punctual representation means being certain about the nature of the emotion perceived. The inherent ambiguity of emotions is not considered here, which might have a negative impact on the accuracy of emotion recognition systems. Gref et al. (2022) analyzed the influence of the ambiguity brought by human annotation in the performance of machine learning models. In their experiments, annotators often combine emotions that are not among the predefined list (e.g., fear and sadness leading to helplessness). This supports their assumption that choosing among the six emotions of Ekman (1992) is not enough to model emotion complexity and that machine learning systems might fail at recognizing the right emotion. Since these results were obtained from a separate analysis of the visual, vocal and textual modalities, a multimodal fusion could perhaps mitigate the ambiguity brought by emotions, hence the motivation for our study.

3.3. Integration of Emotional Ambiguity

There is a growing interest regarding the problem of emotional ambiguity in the affective research community. Some researchers address this issue when implementing their emotion recognition systems (Kim and

Kim, 2018; Fujioka et al., 2020; Li et al., 2021). Sethu et al. (2019) conducted a comprehensive study on introducing ambiguity in the representation of emotions. A summary of the main methods is proposed here.

3.3.1. Discrete Emotions

A second underlying emotion can be identified to complete information on the observed emotion. Vidrascu and Devillers (2005) propose to use major and minor emotions. By extension, an emotional profile can be established where the level of presence of each primary emotion is estimated (Mower et al., 2010). This is a potential solution to the problem outlined by Gref et al. (2022) (cf. section 3.2).

3.3.2. Continuous Emotions

The emotion can be represented using a Gaussian distribution instead of a point (Han et al., 2017): each data sample is associated with the mean and standard deviation of this distribution. Dang et al. (2017) propose not to be restricted to the Gaussian distribution by using a Gaussian mixture model.

4. Multimodal Databases and Representation of Emotion Ambiguity

Databases are the building blocks of the development of emotion recognition systems. Therefore, the choice of the database used for experiments must be thoughtful. If the annotation method does not consider emotional ambiguity, then machine learning models trained on these data will not take it into account either.

Tran et al. (2022) offer a review of multimodal databases with a study of emotion ambiguity in data annotations. They focus on databases which contain facial expression, voice, and text and with English or French as language of speech. They found that among eight reported databases, only CMU-MOSEI (Zadeh et al., 2018b) and CMU-MOSEAS (Zadeh et al., 2020) attempt to represent emotional ambiguity. Both datasets have chosen a discrete model: each data sample is associated with an emotional profile, where a score from 0 to 3 describes the level of presence for each of the six emotions of Ekman (1992). The next section focuses on a review of emotion recognition models trained on CMU-MOSEI (figure 2), a key database in multimodal affective research.

Figure 2: Examples extracted from CMU-MOSEI database (Zadeh et al., 2018b)

5. A Review of Multimodal Emotion Recognition Models

Once a database is chosen, the next step is to design a machine learning model capable of processing annotated data that consider ambiguity, training on them, and recognizing an ambiguous representation of an emotion. In the following, we will focus on the evaluation of the last aspect: the output of the model.

Our review of the multimodal emotion recognition models is comprised of eleven architectures trained on CMU-MOSEI database. All models will be described in subsections 5.1, 5.2, and 5.3. Subsection 5.4 concludes the section with a study of the emotional representations recognized by the models.

5.1. Recurrent Neural Networks

The models falling into this category use either bidirectional, GRU, or LSTM layers (cf. section 2.1). Some perform classification by predicting one or many emotions, others estimate the presence score for each.

5.1.1. Predicting One or More Emotions

Multilogue-Net (Shenoy and Sardana, 2020) is the only reported RNN to predict only one emotion. It uses GRU layers to capture the conversation context and record previous states and emotions while modeling the dependency between interlocutors.

Graph-MFN (Zadeh et al., 2018b) and M3ER (Mittal et al., 2020) both perform binary classification for each emotion. Graph-MFN encodes the three modalities with LSTM layers and uses an interpretable fusion graph to feed its multimodal state memory. This one records the history of interactions between modalities over time. M3ER intends to be robust to noise: it replaces noisy modalities with proxy vectors calculated from the other modalities. Multimodal fusion is done using Memory Fusion Network (Zadeh et al., 2018a), a model with the same architecture as Graph-MFN but with a different fusion module.

5.1.2. Estimating the Presence Score

The two models of this subsection are designed to estimate the intensity of each emotion, rather than detecting the presence of each. The one proposed by Beard et al. (2018) aims to improve Graph-MFN by revisiting the cell memory history of input data encoding layers several times and thus capturing multimodal interactions in the best possible way. With a model training based on L2 loss, their best weighted accuracy is 61.6%.

Williams et al. (2018) attempt to estimate the score of presence with their network composed of bidirectional LSTM layers. Their model is based on early fusion: this means that vectors from audio, image, and text are concatenated before any operation. They perform a custom split 76/14/10 and use a mean absolute error as loss function to select the best model. They obtained a mean unweighted accuracy of 90.6% on the test set.

5.2. Transformer-Based Models

The models of this category use transformers for each modality to extract features. All are designed to predict many emotions (multi-label classification).
MulT (Tsai et al., 2019) is a multimodal fusion model which leverages the benefits of transformers to process unaligned sequences. In the transformer-based joint encoding (TBJE) model by Delbrouck et al. (2020), every modality is encoded jointly before being fed into its respective transformer. Dai et al. (2021) implement a multimodal fusion model able to recognize the emotion directly from raw data. As this can quickly lead to computational overload, an alternative model which inputs the relevant regions of interest extracted from raw data has been developed by the same authors.

5.3. Other Models

Two models using a different architecture are proposed by Lee et al. (2018) and Dai et al. (2020). Both perform classification tasks, the former predicting one emotion and the latter multiple emotions.
Lee et al. (2018) perform multimodal fusion by computing an attention matrix which is the dot product of vocal and textual feature vectors. Their model is composed of three convolutional neural networks: two for vocal and textual feature extraction and one after the attention matrix for the final classification.
Dai et al. (2020) aim to meet the challenges related to unseen or rarely experienced emotions. They built three emotional embedding spaces (textual, visual, and acoustic). Two functions map emotional word embeddings into visual and acoustic spaces. This process can be done for both input data and emotion classes. The final classification is based on the distance between the input sequence and the target emotions. A threshold is set to decide the presence of each emotion.

5.4. Recognizing Emotional Ambiguity

Analyzing the output of an emotion recognition system is a way to study how ambiguity is considered. Out of eleven models, nine consider emotional ambiguity: seven perform multi-label classification and two attempt to estimate the emotion intensity by predicting its presence score. These two models are that of Beard et al. (2018), which attempts to improve Graph-MFN by revisiting the history of cell memories, and the early fusion network of Williams et al. (2018). Since these are recurrent neural networks, they use an activation function that continuously maps to a range of values (e.g., linear, sigmoid) for each output neuron to estimate the presence score of each emotion.
The papers of Dai et al. (2021) and Delbrouck et al. (2020) put together offer a comparison of six out of seven reported models doing multi-label classification: all show similar performance in each of the articles. Unfortunately, we did not find any comparative table of results that involves at least one of the two models which estimate the emotional profile.

6. Discussion

A review of multimodal fusion models for emotion recognition is conducted with a focus on their output. In the case of discrete emotion representation, not considering emotion ambiguity means predicting only one emotion. Two ways to introduce ambiguity would be to predict many emotions and to assess the presence of each emotion (emotional profile). This leads to two different tasks: the former is multi-label classification while the latter is regression for each emotion.
It would have been of interest to compare two models which perform different tasks (predicting one emotion, predicting multiple emotions, or assessing the presence score of each emotion), yet the metrics are not comparable as they all involve different problems.
The main point is that annotations proposed by CMU-MOSEI are not yet fully exploited: many models still perform classification by identifying solely the emotions present in the sample. Therefore, further efforts are needed to assess the intensity of each emotion.

7. Conclusion and Future Work

Developing a multimodal emotion recognition system can be very challenging because of emotion ambiguity arising from human annotation. This can be especially true in a context where many subtle emotions are experienced at the same time in an uncontrolled setting. Emotion ambiguity must first be considered at the level of data annotations and second at every stage of the development of machine learning models, from data preprocessing and model training to final classification.
Among multimodal fusion models trained on a dataset that introduces emotional ambiguity, most perform multi-label classification while a few try to assess the intensity of each emotion. In the next step of our research, we plan to design an emotion recognition system that performs multimodal fusion from visual, vocal, and textual data and is capable of predicting the presence score of each emotion class. The training will be on CMU-MOSEI, a key database for multimodal emotion recognition. Another interesting work would be to analyze the impact of considering ambiguity on the model performance. For instance, there are two ways to address the problem of predicting many emotions: the first by estimating the presence score and setting a threshold to decide which emotions are present and the second by performing binary classification per class (ambiguity less considered than the former).

8. Acknowledgments

This work is done under a CIFRE contract between LIMOS laboratory and Jeolis Solutions company. We thank the National Research and Technology Association (ANRT) for its funding, Ms. Baraa Mohamad and Ms. Lisa Brelet for taking part in the discussions, Mr. Sk. Imran Hossain for English proofreading, and all the members of LIMOS Miners research team for their support.

9. Bibliographical References

Beard, R., Das, R., Ng, R. W. M., Gopalakrishnan, P. G. K., Eerens, L., Swietojanski, P., and Miksik, O. (2018). Multi-modal Sequence Fusion via Recursive Attention for Emotion Recognition. In *Proceedings of the 22nd Conference on Computational Natural Language Learning*, pages 251–259.

Cho, K., van Merriënboer, B., Bahdanau, D., and Bengio, Y. (2014). On the Properties of Neural Machine Translation: Encoder–Decoder Approaches. In *Proceedings of SSST-8, Eighth Workshop on Syntax, Semantics and Structure in Statistical Translation*, pages 103–111.

Dai, W., Liu, Z., Yu, T., and Fung, P. (2020). Modality-Transferable Emotion Embeddings for Low-Resource Multimodal Emotion Recognition. In *Proceedings of the 1st Conference of the Asia-Pacific Chapter of the Association for Computational Linguistics and the 10th International Joint Conference on Natural Language Processing*, pages 269–280.

Dai, W., Cahyawijaya, S., Liu, Z., and Fung, P. (2021). Multimodal End-to-End Sparse Model for Emotion Recognition. pages 5305–5316.

Dang, T., Sethu, V., Epps, J., and Ambikairajah, E. (2017). An Investigation of Emotion Prediction Uncertainty Using Gaussian Mixture Regression. In *INTERSPEECH*, pages 1248–1252.

Delbrouck, J.-B., Tits, N., Brousmiche, M., and Dupont, S. (2020). A Transformer-based joint-encoding for Emotion Recognition and Sentiment Analysis. In *Second Grand-Challenge and Workshop on Multimodal Language (Challenge-HML)*, pages 1–7.

Ekman, P. (1992). An Argument for Basic Emotions. *Cognition & Emotion*, 6(3-4):169–200.

Fujioka, T., Homma, T., and Nagamatsu, K. (2020). Meta-Learning for Speech Emotion Recognition Considering Ambiguity of Emotion Labels. In *INTERSPEECH*, pages 2332–2336.

Gref, M., Matthiesen, N., Venugopala, S. H., Satheesh, S., Vijayananth, A., Ha, D. B., Behnke, S., and Köhler, J. (2022). A Study on the Ambiguity in Human Annotation of German Oral History Interviews for Perceived Emotion Recognition and Sentiment Analysis. *arXiv preprint arXiv:2201.06868*.

Han, J., Zhang, Z., Schmitt, M., Pantic, M., and Schuller, B. (2017). From Hard to Soft: Towards more Human-like Emotion Recognition by Modelling the Perception Uncertainty. In *Proceedings of the 25th ACM international conference on Multimedia*, pages 890–897.

Hochreiter, S. and Schmidhuber, J. (1997). Long Short-Term Memory. *Neural Computation*, 9(8):1735–1780.

Kim, Y. and Kim, J. (2018). Human-Like Emotion Recognition: Multi-Label Learning from Noisy Labeled Audio-Visual Expressive Speech. In *2018 IEEE International Conference on Acoustics, Speech and Signal Processing (ICASSP)*, pages 5104–5108. IEEE.

Lee, C. W., Song, K. Y., Jeong, J., and Choi, W. Y. (2018). Convolutional Attention Networks for Multimodal Emotion Recognition from Speech and Text Data. In *Proceedings of the First Grand Challenge and Workshop on Human Multimodal Language (Challenge-HML)*, pages 28–34.

Li, Z., Xie, H., Cheng, G., and Li, Q. (2021). Word-level Emotion Distribution with Two Schemas for Short Text Emotion Classification. *Knowledge-Based Systems*, 227:107163.

Mittal, T., Bhattacharya, U., Chandra, R., Bera, A., and Manocha, D. (2020). M3ER: Multiplicative multimodal emotion recognition using facial, textual, and speech cues. *AAAI 2020 - 34th AAAI Conference on Artificial Intelligence*, pages 1359–1367.

Mower, E., Matarić, M. J., and Narayanan, S. (2010). A Framework for Automatic Human Emotion Classification Using Emotion Profiles. *IEEE Transactions on Audio, Speech, and Language Processing*, 19(5):1057–1070.

Plutchik, R. (2001). The Nature of Emotions: Human emotions have deep evolutionary roots, a fact that may explain their complexity and provide tools for clinical practice. *American Scientist*, 89(4):344–350.

Russell, J. A. and Mehrabian, A. (1977). Evidence for a Three-Factor Theory of Emotions. *Journal of Research in Personality*, 11(3):273–294.

Schlosberg, H. (1954). Three dimensions of emotion. *Psychological review*, 61(2):81.

Schuster, M. and Paliwal, K. K. (1997). Bidirectional recurrent neural networks. *IEEE transactions on Signal Processing*, 45(11):2673–2681.

Sethu, V., Provost, E. M., Epps, J., Busso, C., Cummins, N., and Narayanan, S. (2019). The Ambiguous World of Emotion Representation. *arXiv preprint arXiv:1909.00360*.

Shenoy, A. and Sardana, A. (2020). Multilogue-Net: A Context-Aware RNN for Multi-modal Emotion Detection and Sentiment Analysis in Conversation. In *Second Grand-Challenge and Workshop on Multimodal Language (Challenge-HML)*, pages 19–28.

Tran, H., Brelet, L., Falih, I., Goblet, X., and Mephu Nguifo, E. (2022). L'ambiguïté dans la représentation des émotions : état de l'art des bases de données multimodales. *Revue des Nouvelles Technologies de l'Information*, Extraction et Gestion des Connaissances, RNTI-E-38:87–98.

Tsai, Y.-H. H., Bai, S., Liang, P. P., Kolter, J. Z., Morency, L.-P., and Salakhutdinov, R. (2019). Multimodal Transformer for Unaligned Multimodal Language Sequences. In *Proceedings of the conference. Association for Computational Linguistics. Meeting*, volume 2019, page 6558. NIH Public Access.

Vaswani, A., Shazeer, N., Parmar, N., Uszkoreit, J.,

Jones, L., Gomez, A. N., Kaiser, Ł., and Polosukhin, I. (2017). Attention Is All You Need. *Advances in Neural Information Processing Systems*, 30.

Vidrascu, L. and Devillers, L. (2005). Real-life Emotion Representation and Detection in Call Centers Data. In *International Conference on Affective Computing and Intelligent Interaction*, pages 739–746. Springer.

Williams, J., Kleinegesse, S., Comanescu, R., and Radu, O. (2018). Recognizing Emotions in Video Using Multimodal DNN Feature Fusion. In *Proceedings of the First Grand Challenge and Workshop on Human Multimodal Language (Challenge-HML)*, pages 11–19.

Zadeh, A., Liang, P. P., Mazumder, N., Poria, S., Cambria, E., and Morency, L.-P. (2018a). Memory Fusion Network for Multi-View Sequential Learning. In *Proceedings of the AAAI Conference on Artificial Intelligence*, volume 32.

Zadeh, A. B., Liang, P. P., Vanbriesen, J., Poria, S., Tong, E., Cambria, E., Chen, M., and Morency, L.-P. (2018b). Multimodal Language Analysis in the Wild: CMU-MOSEI Dataset and Interpretable Dynamic Fusion Graph. In *Proceedings of the 56th Annual Meeting of the Association for Computational Linguistics*, pages 2236–2246.

Zadeh, A. B., Cao, Y. S., Hessner, S., Liang, P. P., Poria, S., and Morency, L.-P. (2020). CMU-MOSEAS: A Multimodal Language Dataset for Spanish, Portuguese, German and French. In *Proceedings of the 2020 Conference on Empirical Methods in Natural Language Processing*, pages 1801–1812.

Proceedings of the workshop on People in Vision, Language, and the Mind @LREC2022, pages 12–16
Marseille, 20 June 2022
© European Language Resources Association (ELRA), licensed under CC-BY-NC-4.0

Development of a MultiModal Annotation Framework and Dataset for Deep Video Understanding

Erika Loc†, Keith Curtis*, George Awad*‡, Shahzad Rajput*‡, Ian Soboroff*
Montgomery College†, National Institute of Standards and Technology*, Georgetown University‡
Maryland, USA
x.erika.loc@gmail.com, {keith.curtis, george.awad, shahzad.rajput, ian.soboroff}@nist.gov

Abstract

In this paper we introduce our approach and methods for collecting and annotating a new dataset for deep video understanding. The proposed dataset is composed of 3 seasons (15 episodes) of the BBC Land Girls TV Series in addition to 14 Creative Common movies with total duration of 28.5 hr. The main contribution of this paper is a novel annotation framework on the movie and scene levels to support an automatic query generation process that can capture the high-level movie features (e.g. how characters and locations are related to each other) as well as fine grained scene-level features (e.g. character interactions, natural language descriptions, and sentiments). Movie-level annotations include constructing a global static knowledge graph (KG) to capture major relationships, while the scene-level annotations include constructing a sequence of knowledge graphs (KGs) to capture fine-grained features. The annotation framework supports generating multiple query types. The objective of the framework is to provide a guide to annotating long duration videos to support tasks and challenges in the video and multimedia understanding domains. These tasks and challenges can support testing automatic systems on their ability to learn and comprehend a movie or long video in terms of actors, entities, events, interactions and their relationship to each other.

Keywords: Dataset, Multimodal, Multimedia, Annotation Framework, Video Understanding

1. Introduction

In this paper we use the term Deep Video Understanding (DVU) to refer to the ability of making sense of and understanding long duration videos with a self contained storyline such as movies and TV series. This is a difficult challenge requiring a suitable dataset which has been annotated to both the entire movie and to the individual scene level. Such a dataset must include annotations of characters & entities, as well as relationships and interactions between these, chronological ordering of such interactions, scene sentiment annotations, and natural language descriptions of individual scenes.

As this research is performed over the whole movie and individual scenes, the development of this dataset is separated into these two distinct parts to support different requirements. The whole-movie annotations support research on the movie level for the extraction of all main characters, entities, and relationships between them. Scene-level annotations support research on the scene level for the extraction of characters in each scene, interactions between characters, and the chronological order of interactions.

In this paper we describe the construction of such a corpus to support this research. Our corpus consists of all 15 episodes from the BBC TV series *Land Girls*[1], and 14 Creative Commons (CC) licensed movies.

The remainder of this paper is structured as follows: Related work is discussed in Section 2. Section 3 describes the dataset in detail. Full descriptions of the annotation framework are provided in section 4, while supported query types are explained in section 5. Finally we discuss how this annotation efforts were utilized in public multimedia grand challenges in section 6.

[1] https://www.bbc.co.uk/programmes/b00xxnhv/episodes/guide

2. Related Work

MovieQA (Tapaswi et al., 2016) is a dataset which aims to evaluate automatic story comprehension from video and text. It consists of 14,944 multiple choice questions, each with 5 multiple-choice answers, with one of these being the correct answer, from about 408 movies with high semantic diversity. Movies were segmented into video clips with a maximum duration of 200 seconds where participants have to answer a question related to the clip. The dataset itself comes with multiple answering sources for questions such as plot synopses, scripts, subtitles, and audio descriptions. The plot synopses was used by annotators to come up with questions and answers rather than watching the whole movie.

The *MovieGraphs* dataset (Vicol et al., 2018) provides detailed graph-based annotations of social situations depicted in movie clips. Annotations are provided for characters in each clip, their emotional and physical attributes, and relationships and interactions between characters.

In (Lei et al., 2020) work, the authors collected 108,965 queries on 21,793 videos from 6 TV shows where queries can target the visual or subtitle modalities. Queries are textual and only target specific moments in the TV show.

Early visions of video understanding (Debattista et al., 2018) explored the usage of visual and audio descriptors, in addition to employing semantic analysis and linking with external knowledge sources in order to populate a knowledge graph.

High-level Video Understanding *(HLVU)* (Curtis et al., 2020a) describes a vision for video understanding over the whole movie level. Knowledge Graph annotations were used to describe the overall storyline of movies and characters contained within. A challenge was run testing systems on their ability to understand movies at a high-level over the whole movie. The first workshop on HLVU (Cur-

tis et al., 2020b) challenged participant systems to extract, understand, and answer queries over the full movie.
In this work our contribution is the development of an annotation framework for the specific task of Deep Video Understanding - making sense of movies, the characters there within, and the relationships and interactions between such. The work presented in this paper extends the HLVU work deeper to the scene-level, thereby requiring the development of a suitable dataset, segmented to the scene-level, and annotated over the whole movie and the scene-level.

3. Dataset

In order to undertake this new research area, there was a critical need to identify a representative dataset to work with and be able to distribute it to researchers as most of the available datasets in the computer vision and video analysis domains are not suitable due to various reasons such as lack of properly licensed free open movies, most available video datasets are either from social media user uploads, or covering specific application domains such as surveillance, action and activity detection, etc. To tackle this problem, the authors applied two approaches to recruit datasets: a) searching for Creative Common (CC) (Creative Commons, 2019) movies publicly available, b) reaching out to big broadcasting companies to license TV Series. The following sections explain these two efforts and their datasets characteristics.

3.1. Creative Common Movies

The most important criteria in selecting the movies of the dataset were reasonable video quality, duration of more than 15 min at least, and self contained story lines with clear actors, relations, events and entities. In total, a dataset of 14 movies (17.5 hrs) has been collected from public websites such as Vimeo[2], the Internet Archive[3] and YouTube[4]. Table 1 shows the current set of collected movies, their genre and durations. All movies have been deemed by the authors to be suitable for this research.

3.2. Licensed TV Series

The authors have also been in deliberations with the BBC regarding the licensing of the TV show *Land Girls* for use in this dataset. This is a 3-season / 15-episode series set in World War 2 about the lives of a group of women doing their part for Britain in the *Women's Land Army* during the war. Each episode is about 45 mins long and the whole 3-season set is about 11 hrs. Automatic audio transcripts were also provided by the BBC with the series. This paper presents our efforts annotating the first 2 seasons of Land Girls series.

3.3. Dataset characteristics

In order to highlight some content characteristics for both types of data we collected, table 2 shows the total number of scenes, entities (key characters and locations), unique relationships between either characters and each other or characters and locations, and finally interactions between characters. We differentiate between actions and interactions in this work by restricting interactions to be between people (e.g. talking with), while actions can be done solely by individual character (e.g. running). In the presented annotations framework we focused more on interactions.

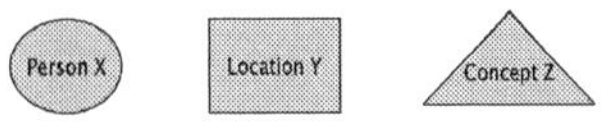

Figure 1: Node Shapes in Movie-level KG. In this context the word person and character are used interchangeably

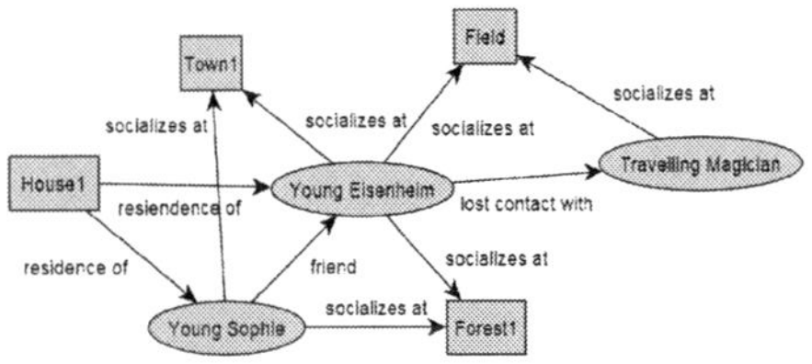

Figure 2: Movie-level KG

4. Annotation Framework

Our annotators created datasets for each film at the movie-level and the scene-level, both focusing to capture their own details from the films. Annotation at either the movie or scene level requires first that the annotator watch the film all of the way through to gain a general understanding of the story. During this stage our annotators make mental note of all of the locations and which characters and entities are relevant to the overall plot of the film as not every character or entity that appears in the film is documented in the datasets at the movie-level. When annotating at the movie-level, our annotators utilized yEd Graph Editor[5], a general-purpose diagramming tool to exhibit the relationships between locations, characters, and concepts. For scene-level annotations, we created an internal annotation tool to be employed for the process. This annotation tool was written in HTML/CSS and JavaScript, and is a combination of two pre-existing tools. Necessary components and features from both sources were integrated into the final tool. Such features include a snapshot saver to capture images of key characters and locations directly from the films, a canvas tool to create knowledge graphs (KGs), and a scene selection area to navigate between scenes. Some newly integrated components consist of a right-click menu for labeling nodes within the knowledge graph (KG), a text area to add natural language descriptions, as well as save buttons to save the knowledge graph and text area's contents locally. The vocabulary[6] that is used in the knowledge graphs at both the movie and scene level, aside from

[2]https://vimeo.com/
[3]https://archive.org/
[4]https://www.youtube.com/
[5]https://www.yworks.com/
[6]https://www-nlpir.nist.gov/projects/trecvid/dvu/training/vocab.dvu.json

Movie	Genre	Duration
Honey	Romance	86 min
Let's Bring Back Sophie	Drama	50 min
Nuclear Family	Drama	28 min
Shooters	Drama	41 min
Spiritual Contact The Movie	Fantasy	66 min
Super Hero	Fantasy	18 min
The Adventures of Huckleberry Finn	Adventure	106 min
The Big Something	Comedy	101 min
Time Expired	Comedy / Drama	92 min
Valkaama	Adventure	93 min
Bagman	Drama / Thriller	107 min
Manos	Horror	73 min
Road to Bali	Comedy / Musical	90 min
The Illusionist	Adventure / Drama	109 min

Table 1: The DVU Dataset of 14 open source movies

entity names, are derived from a predetermined ontology in order to prevent disparity within the data. This vocabulary included classes of relationships (social, family, work-related, person-place), locations, sentiments, interactions, and emotions. Overall, each movie was annotated by only 1 annotator while Land Girls TV series was all annotated by a summer student for a duration of about 5 month. In total we hired 6 annotators and they were all given 1-2 hrs training sessions to describe the purpose and usage of the tool. The following two subsections provide more details about the movie-level and scene-level annotations.

4.1. Movie-level Annotations

The yEd graph editor is used to document the film at the movie-level or as a whole. Nodes in different shapes as illustrated in figure 1 are used to distinguish between various movie elements with rectangles representing locations, ellipses for characters, and triangle for concepts. Concepts are used to highlight dominant ideas that play a major role in any movie and usually one or more key characters are involved into engaging with such ideas (e.g. bad dream, imaginary figure, etc). Figure 2 exhibits an example of the movie level knowledge graphs (KGs). Rays connecting the nodes depict the relationship between each entity the characters interact with and the locations they appear in. The final output knowledge graph are saved by annotators as xgml file storing all data structure needed to reconstruct the graph in the future if needed to do any updates.

4.2. Scene-level Annotations

Once the whole-movie annotations have been recorded, our annotators move onto documenting the film at the scene-level with the annotation tool created internally. Figure 4 shows the interface of the web tool used for scene annotation. The films are segmented into scenes each lasting roughly 20 seconds to 2 minutes long. Using the scene selector on the tool to navigate from scene to scene, the film is re-watched to observe more in-depth details not included in the knowledge graphs (KGs) created at the movie-level. Snapshots of each location, relevant character, and entity are captured throughout the scenes. Ideally 5 or more images of each, captured at various angles to ensure variety amongst the snapshots are saved across the entire film. Cataloging of relationships and interactions between each of the characters & entities within each scene is done in the canvas of the annotation tool. Similar to the whole-movie annotations, different shapes represent individual aspects as shown in Figure 3. A sample knowledge graph (KG) is shown in Figure 5 illustrating all interactions taking place in chronological order. The text description for the same scene is shown in figure 6. It can be shown how both the text description and scene graph both complements each other. Each scene knowledge graph is finally saved as a json file to store all node information and links between nodes and each other.

Dataset	Scenes	Entities	Relations	Interactions
Movies	621	1572	650	2491
TV Series	422	390	711	1622

Table 2: Dataset content of scenes, entities (characters, locations, & concepts), relationships between entities, and interactions between characters

5. Query Design and Generation

A set of queries were designed to test participating systems on their understanding of the test movies at the movie-level and the scene-level. Movie-level queries asked three main sets of questions: Multiple choice questions on the part of Knowledge Graph for selected movies, possible path analysis between selected persons / entities of interest in a movie, and Fill in the Blank Space, in which systems were asked to fill in the graph space for a partial Knowledge Graph of movies. Scene-level queries asked five main sets of questions: Find the next / previous interaction, Find the unique scene, Match selected scenes with natural language descriptions, Fill in the graph space, and Match scenes with scene sentiment labels.

The majority of queries on both the movie-level and the scene-level were generated automatically. Additional queries which required human generation were: Path analysis questions on the movie-level, Match scenes with description on the scene-level, and Match scenes with sentiment labels on the scene-level.

For generating path analysis questions, two character nodes on the movie-level KG were chosen for each question which had an indirect connecting path between them. For match scene-description questions, scene descriptions and KG's were analysed and scenes and related descriptions considered to be sufficiently different were chosen. Similarly for matching scenes with sentiments, scene KG's and sentiment labels sufficiently different were chosen.

Figure 3: Web tool interface for scene-level annotations

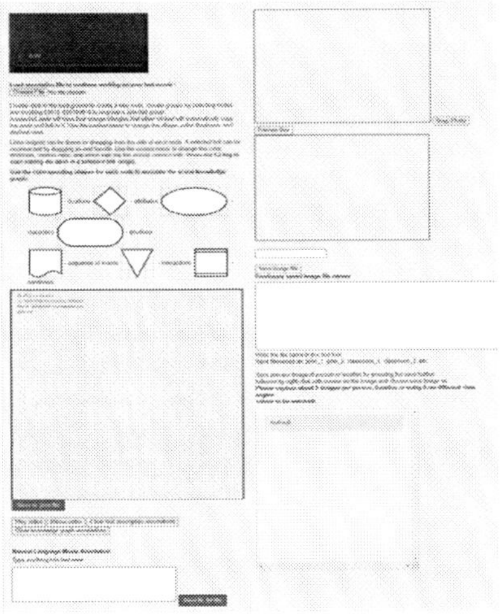

Figure 4: Web tool interface for scene-level annotations

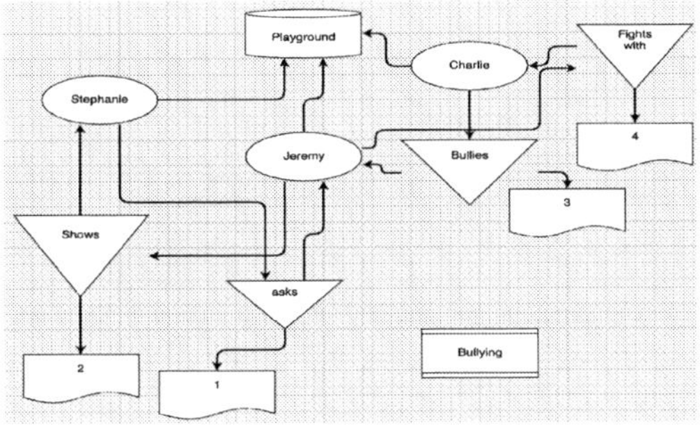

Figure 5: Scene-level KG

The bell rings for recess and Jeremy is sitting on the bench by the playground reading a comic book. Stephanie runs by but comes back to talk to Jeremy. She sits down on the bench next to him, and they discuss comics while he shows her his comic book. Charlie Luther walks up and grabs it from Jeremy's hands.and rips it up. Jeremy gathers the ripped pages from the ground and Stephanie stands up for him. Jeremy imagines the Great Celestial shows up to save the day. But in reality, he shoves Charlie to the ground out of anger then faints. Stephanie calls for Ms. Johnson.

Figure 6: Scene text description sample

6. Discussion and Conclusion

The described annotation framework was followed and used to generate queries to support the deep video understanding ACM Multimedia Grand Challenge in 2020 and 2021[7], as well as the ACM Multimedia Asia Grand Challenge in 2021[8]. In these challenges the participants were given the original whole movies, snapshot images for key characters and location entities, the ontology of relationships, sentiments, interactions, locations and character emotional status. The annotated dataset was divided into training and testing sets. In 2021 the training set consisted of 10 movies, while participants were tested on 4 movies. The provided training set additionally contained the movie-level and scene-level knowledge graphs and scene text descriptions. We should note here that unfortunately the Land Girls TV series videos couldn't be distributed due to lack of time in securing the hosting agreement between the BBC and the hosting university. However, all annotations are now public and available for researchers [9].

In total, 6 systems (Yu et al., 2020), (Baumgartner et al., 2020), (Anand et al., 2020),(Zhang et al., 2021b),(Anand et al., 2021),(Zhang et al., 2021a) submitted solutions in the two years combined. Based on these two grand challenge results, we observed that systems tend to perform better on scene-level queries compared to movie-level. This could be due to the scene specific queries such as interactions between two specific characters or the sentiment of a given scene. On the other hand the hardest movie-level query is the path analysis between two characters or in other words how is character X related to character Y which requires correctly representing the movie relationships and understanding in higher level how the whole movie storyline unravels.

To conclude, in this paper we introduced our new dataset of movies and TV series and explained how we developed a novel annotation framework to describe each movie or episode at two levels. First, a global level using a static knowledge graph to represent how each entity is related to each other, and second at a more fine-grained level per scene to capture interactions, sentiments and other scene characteristics. The framework supports automatic query generation to test systems on various visual and non-visual facets and their ability to comprehend a visual storyline with many characters, relationships and locations. As this domain is gaining attention and more research groups are looking into how to apply multimodal integration techniques to process visual, audio and textual information channels, we anticipate the need for similar annotation frameworks and datasets to support these research efforts.

7. Acknowledgements

All the work presented in this paper is supported by the National Institute of Standards and Technology, Information Technology Laboratory, Information Access Division.

[7]https://sites.google.com/view/dvuchallenge2021/home/

[8]https://sites.google.com/view/dvu-asia-challenge-2021

[9]https://ir.nist.gov/Landgirls.Challenge/landgirls.html

Disclaimer: Certain commercial entities, equipment, or materials may be identified in this document in order to describe an experimental procedure or concept adequately. Such identification is not intended to imply recommendation or endorsement by the National Institute of Standards and Technology, nor is it intended to imply that the entities, materials, or equipment are necessarily the best available for the purpose. The views and conclusions contained herein are those of the authors and should not be interpreted as necessarily representing the official policies or endorsements, either expressed or implied, of NIST, or the U.S. Government.

8. Bibliographical References

Anand, V., Ramesh, R., Wang, Z., Feng, Y., Feng, J., Lyu, W., Zhu, T., Yuan, S., and Lin, C.-Y., (2020). *Story Semantic Relationships from Multimodal Cognitions*, page 4650–4654. Association for Computing Machinery, New York, NY, USA.

Anand, V., Ramesh, R., Jin, B., Wang, Z., Lei, X., and Lin, C.-Y., (2021). *MultiModal Language Modelling on Knowledge Graphs for Deep Video Understanding*. Association for Computing Machinery, New York, NY, USA.

Baumgartner, M., Rossetto, L., and Bernstein, A., (2020). *Towards Using Semantic-Web Technologies for Multi-Modal Knowledge Graph Construction*, page 4645–4649. Association for Computing Machinery, New York, NY, USA.

Creative Commons. (2019). About the licenses. `https://creativecommons.org/licenses/`, Last accessed on 2019-11-06.

Curtis, K., Awad, G., Rajput, S., and Soboroff, I. (2020a). Hlvu: A new challenge to test deep understanding of movies the way humans do. In *Proceedings of the 2020 International Conference on Multimedia Retrieval*, pages 355–361.

Curtis, K., Awad, G., Rajput, S., and Soboroff, I. (2020b). International workshop on deep video understanding. In *Proceedings of the 2020 International Conference on Multimodal Interaction*, pages 871–873.

Debattista, J., Salim, F. A., Haider, F., Conran, C., Conlan, O., Curtis, K., Wei, W., Junior, A. C., and O'Sullivan, D. (2018). Expressing multimedia content using semantics—a vision. In *2018 IEEE 12th International Conference on Semantic Computing (ICSC)*, pages 302–303. IEEE.

Lei, J., Yu, L., Berg, T. L., and Bansal, M. (2020). Tvr: A large-scale dataset for video-subtitle moment retrieval. In *European Conference on Computer Vision*, pages 447–463. Springer.

Tapaswi, M., Zhu, Y., Stiefelhagen, R., Torralba, A., Urtasun, R., and Fidler, S. (2016). Movieqa: Understanding stories in movies through question-answering. In *Proceedings of the IEEE conference on computer vision and pattern recognition*, pages 4631–4640.

Vicol, P., Tapaswi, M., Castrejon, L., and Fidler, S. (2018). Moviegraphs: Towards understanding human-centric situations from videos. In *Proceedings of the IEEE Conference on Computer Vision and Pattern Recognition*, pages 8581–8590.

Yu, F., Wang, D., Zhang, B., and Ren, T., (2020). *Deep Relationship Analysis in Video with Multimodal Feature Fusion*, page 4640–4644. Association for Computing Machinery, New York, NY, USA.

Zhang, B., Yu, F., Fang, Y., Ren, T., and Wu, G. (2021a). Hybrid improvements in multimodal analysis for deep video understanding.

Zhang, B., Yu, F., Gao, Y., Ren, T., and Wu, G., (2021b). *Joint Learning for Relationship and Interaction Analysis in Video with Multimodal Feature Fusion*, page 4848–4852. Association for Computing Machinery, New York, NY, USA.

Proceedings of the workshop on People in Vision, Language, and the Mind @LREC2022 , pages 17–25
Marseille, 20 June 2022
© European Language Resources Association (ELRA), licensed under CC-BY-NC-4.0

Cognitive States and Types of Nods

Taiga Mori*†, Kristiina Jokinen†, Yasuharu Den‡
*Graduate School of Science and Engineering, Chiba University
‡Graduate School of Humanities, Chiba University
1-33 Yayoicho, Inage-ku, Chiba 263-8522, Japan

†AI Research Center, AIST Tokyo Waterfront
2-4-7 Aomi, Koto-ku, Tokyo 135-0064, Japan

Abstract
In this paper we will study how different types of nods are related to the cognitive states of the listener. The distinction is made between nods with movement starting upwards (up-nods) and nods with movement starting downwards (down-nods) as well as between single or repetitive nods. The data is from Japanese multiparty conversations, and the results accord with the previous findings indicating that up-nods are related to the change in the listener's cognitive state after hearing the partner's contribution, while down-nods convey the meaning that the listener's cognitive state is not changed.

Keywords: head nod, multimodal interaction, human-agent interaction

1. Introduction

When a speaker is speaking, the interlocuters do not only listen to the presentation, but simultaneously give feedback to the speaker with the help of short utterances, head nods, or sometimes both. Such feedback giving behaviors convey various meanings such as acknowledgement, understanding, agreement and empathy, and they are necessary for smooth interaction. In order to support natural interaction with the user, conversational agents should also exhibit similar behavior with appropriate features and appropriate timing, as well as the capability to recognize the user's behavior to confirm their interest in the ongoing topic or that they have understood what the agent said (cf. Jokinen, 2018).

Many studies have focused on nodding which is generally considered one of the most important and natural feedback signals in human-human conversations. Besides the form and function of nodding in giving and eliciting feedback (see e.g., Navarretta et al., 2012), also the timing when the listener produces a nod is important; for instance, Watanabe and Yuuki (1989) proposed a model to predict listener's nod timing from speech input of preceding utterance, and Yatsuka et al. (1997; 1998) and Watanabe et al. (2004) implemented the model in real and virtual robots.

However, in human-agent interaction studies nods are often defined as vertical head movements in general, and the meaning differences that are conveyed in the forms of the nods are ignored. For instance, it is shown that nods can be classified into two types based on the direction of the initial movement, up-nods and down-nods. Boholm & Allwood (2010) noticed that up-nods and down-nods are likely to co-occur with different vocal feedback expressions in Swedish, while Navaretta et al. (2012) compared the use of up-nods and down-nods in Danish, Swedish and Finnish and reported several differences in the frequency of nods in these languages. It is interesting that although Nordic countries are culturally similar, the study found that e.g., Danes use down-nods much more frequently than Swedes and Finns, whereas Swedes use up-nods significantly more often than Danes and slightly more often than Finns. Moreover, it was observed that up-nods are used as acknowledgement for new information in Swedish. In a closer study of nods in the Finnish language, Toivio & Jokinen (2012) reported that up-nods and down-nods have different functions in the construction of the shared understanding among the speakers, and that up-nods seem to mark the preceding information as surprise or unexpected to the listener, while down-nods confirm the information as expected, and signal the partner to continue their presentation.

Although the distinction between up-nods and down-nods seems to be functionally appropriate in a wide variety of culturally and linguistically different languages, we wish to confirm that the distinction also works in different languages. Thus, in this paper, we investigate how up-nods and down-nods are used as feedback in Japanese conversations and aim to verify if a similar distinction exists in Japanese as in the Nordic languages. Finally, we sketch a model of nod production for conversational agents.

The organization of this paper is as follows. In section 2, we describe our data and method to identify up-nods and down-nods. In section 3, we conduct quantitative analysis and calculate correlations between feedback expressions and the two types of nods. In section 4, we conduct qualitative analysis and precisely examine when and how up-nods are used in conversations. In section 5, we discuss the results of quantitative and qualitative analysis, and based on that, we propose a model of nod production for conversational agents in section 6. Finally, we describe our future work in section 7.

2. Data and Method

2.1 Data

The data is Chiba three-party conversation corpus (Den & Enomoto, 2007). This corpus contains a collection of 3 party conversations by friends of graduate and undergraduate students. Figure 1 shows the settings of the conversation. Participants sat at regular intervals and were recorded by cameras installed in front of each participant and an outside position where everyone can be seen. In addition, each participant's audio was recorded by the headset. In this corpus, the topic of the conversation is randomly determined by a dice such as "angry story" and "stinking story", and the participants freely talked about that. We used all 12 conversations in the corpus for this study, thus, the total number of participants is 36. The duration of each conversation is 9 and a half minutes, and the total duration of the conversations is 114 minutes. This corpus also contains annotations of morphological and prosodic information, response tokens (Den et al., 2011), head gestures (nod, shake and the others) and so on. We used these existing annotations for the following analysis.

Figure 1: The settings of the conversations

2.2 Identification of Nod Type

According to head gesture annotation, the data contains a total of 2336 nods produced either by the speaker and the listener. We classified them into up-nods and down-nods. As to the definition of the nod type, we followed previous studies and identified them based on the direction of the initial movement. In this study, we used automatic face recognition and automatically classified all nods into the two types. The classification procedure is as follows. First, we conducted face recognition for all frames of videos recorded from the front of participants and estimated the face position in the image. Here, we used OpenCV detector (OpenCV, 2020) learned on frontal face. Second, we smoothed time-series data of vertical face position with moving average filter and normalized it by standardization. The window size of moving average filter is empirically determined to be 7. Finally, we classified all nods into up-nods or down-nods based on whether or not the face is rising in the first 10 frames immediately after the start of the nod. Figure 2 shows examples of trajectories of up-nods and down-nods.

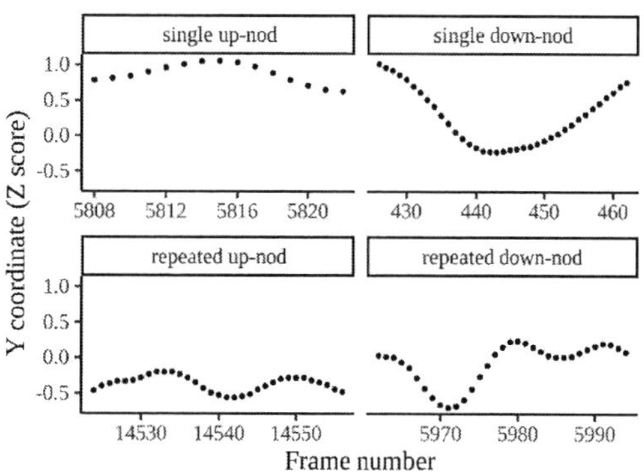

Figure 2: Trajectories of up-nods and down-nods

3. Quantitative Analysis

3.1 Purpose

Previous studies focusing on feedback behaviors in Nordic countries analyzed correlations between the two types of nods and feedback expressions and reported that up-nods are used as acknowledgement for new information in Swedish and Finnish. We also analyzed the correlations between the two types of nods and feedback expressions in Japanese. Our hypothesis is that if up-nods are used as acknowledgement for new information, they should be likely to co-occur with feedback expressions considered as "change of state tokens" (Heritage, 1984). According to Heritage (1984), change of state tokens suggest "its producer has undergone some kind of change in his or her locally current state of knowledge, information, orientation or awareness" (p. 299). Considering Japanese change of state tokens, Tanaka (2010) noted that Japanese particles *aa, ee, haa, huun, hee* and *hoo* have similar functions with English change of state token *oh*. Endo (2018) distinguished *a* and *aa* as change of state tokens and noted that *aa* is used when its producer has prior knowledge of the preceding information, while *a* is used when he or she has no knowledge. If the listener acknowledges preceding information as new, he or she would use these tokens in concurrence with up-nods.

3.2 Method

In this analysis, we analyze the correlations between the two types of nods and feedback expressions. First, we defined and extracted feedback expressions from the data. However, this is not so easy because some expressions such as "yes" are used as both an answer as well as feedback. In our data, response expressions are annotated with form tags and position tags defined by Den et al. (2011), and they are useful to determine whether the expression is an answer or feedback. With these tags, we excluded expressions occurred in the first or second pair part of an adjacency pair and unclassified positions such as after a long silence because they are not feedback to other participant's utterance. We also restricted our targets to responsive interjections, expressive interjections and lexical reactive expressions. Second, we extracted the two types of nods overlapping with these feedback expressions. We excluded data if the gap between starting times of the feedback expression and nod exceeds 200 msec because they are likely to be responses to different objects that are temporally adjacent in the speaker's utterance. Finally, we calculated each participant's ratios of the two types of nods with respect to co-occurring feedback expressions. Table 1 shows all feedback expressions co-occurred with up-nods and down-nods in the data. Note that, when consecutive expressions belong to same form, we treated them as one expression (e.g., "maa un" = "maaun").

Expression	Explanation
a (oh)	Expressive interjection to express a surprise or notice.
aa (ah)	Expressive interjection to express a surprise or notice.
aan (ah)	One of the derived forms of *aa*. Perhaps fusion of *aa* and *un*.
ee (really)	Expressive interjection to express a surprise or notice. It expresses stronger

	unexpectedness than *a* and *aa*, and therefore sometimes implies negative meanings such as aversion or disappointment.
haa (oh)	Expressive interjection to express an admiration.
hai (yes)	Responsive interjection to express an acceptance of other's utterance. It is used similarly to *un* but is more formal than *un*.
hee (oh)	Expressive interjection to express a surprise, notice or admiration.
hoo (oh)	Expressive interjection to express a surprise, notice or admiration.
huun (uh-huh)	Expressive interjection to express a surprise, notice or admiration. It is sometimes perceived as a lukewarm reaction.
maane (yeah)	Lexical reactive expression to express an understanding or agreement to other's opinion or assertion. Fusion of *maa* and *ne*. *maa* is also used as filler and therefore sometimes implies hesitation.
maaun (yeah)	Lexical reactive expression to express an understanding or agreement to other's opinion or assertion. Fusion of *maa* and *un*. *maa* is also used as filler and therefore sometimes implies hesitation.
n (yeah)	Responsive interjection to express an acceptance of other's utterance. Abbreviation of *un*.
na (yeah)	Lexical reactive expression to express an agreement to other's opinion or assertion.
naruhodone (I see)	Lexical reactive expression to express an understanding to other's opinion or assertion. Fusion of *naruhodo* and *ne*.
ne (yeah)	Lexical reactive expression to express an agreement to other's opinion or assertion.
oo (oh)	Expressive interjection to express a surprise, notice or admiration. It is used when the provided information is socially or personally desirable.
soo (yeah)	Lexical reactive expression to express an agreement to other's opinion or assertion.
sooka (I see)	Lexical reactive expression to express an understanding to other's opinion or assertion. Fusion of *soo* and final particle *ka*.
soone (yeah)	Lexical reactive expression to express an agreement to other's opinion or assertion. Fusion of *soo* and *ne*.
un (yeah)	Responsive interjection to express an acceptance of other's utterance.
uun ↑ (oh)	Expressive interjection to express a surprise, notice or admiration.
uun ↓ (yeah)	Responsive interjection to express an acceptance of other's utterance. Perhaps one of the derived forms of *un*.

Table 1: All feedback expressions co-occurred with up-nods and down-nods

3.3 Results and Discussion

Figure 3 shows the ratios of up-nods and down-nods with respect to co-occurring feedback expressions. Error bars show standard errors, and "×2" and "×3+" next to the expressions mean "repeated twice" and "repeated more than three times" respectively. First, the figure shows, as we predicted, up-nods co-occurred with change of state tokens *a, aa, ee, haa*×2, *hee* and *hoo* more frequently than down-nods; there is, however, no big difference between them in *aa*×3+, *haa, haa*×3+ and *huun*; and the tendency is inversed in only *aa*×2. These results are consistent with our hypothesis. Moreover, comparing *a* and *aa*, *a* co-occurred with up-nods more frequently than *aa*, which is consistent with the difference between *a* and *aa* observed by Endo (2018). Since *aa* is used when the listener has prior knowledge of the preceding informing, it is more likely to co-occur with down-nods than *a*. On the other hand, *huun* and single and repeated *haa* particles do not have clear tendency. As for the character of *huun*, Tanaka (2010) described that it is displaying involvement in ongoing talk without topical engagement. In other words, *huun* is used when the listener acknowledges the information as new but do not have interest in that, and this seems to be applied to *haa* as well. This fact suggests that *huun* and *haa* are not likely to co-occur with up-nods because cognitive change is not big when the information is just new but not interesting.

The figure also shows that *ne* co-occurred with down-nods more frequently than up-nods. As for the character of *ne* as sentence final particle, Kamio (1994) argued from the viewpoint of the theory of territory of information that a part of *ne* ("obligatory *ne*" as Kamio called) is used when the speaker assumes that (1) the information falls into both speaker and listener's territory or (2) that the information falls completely into the listener's territory and partially into the speaker's territory; thus, *ne* is used to seek assent, confirmation and reconfirmation. In other words, *ne* is used by a speaker when he or she assumes that the listener has same level or more detailed information about it. Even though Kamio (1994) argued about only *ne* produced by speakers, this particle is often used by listeners as well when the speaker has used it in the immediate context; for instance, "*Kyoo wa ii tenki da ne* (Today's weather is good, isn't it?)" followed by "*Ne* (Yeah.)". Applying above Kamio's notions (1) and (2) to listener's *ne*, it is assumed that both speaker and listener use ne only when they have same level of information because (2) cannot hold in the speaker side and the listener side at the same time. Therefore, when the listener uses *ne*, preceding information is not new for him or her, and the speaker also does not expect the listener receives the information as such.

Another interesting point is that *un* co-occurred with down-nods more frequently than up-nods when it is single occurrence, but this tendency gradually becomes inversed as the number of repetition increases. In general, single *un* is used as a continuer (Schegloff, 1982) or usual acknowledgement. On the other hand, repeated *un* is used to display one's agreement or understanding to the preceding utterance. Therefore, when the listener uses repeated *un*, he or she may have undergone a change in his or her cognitive state.

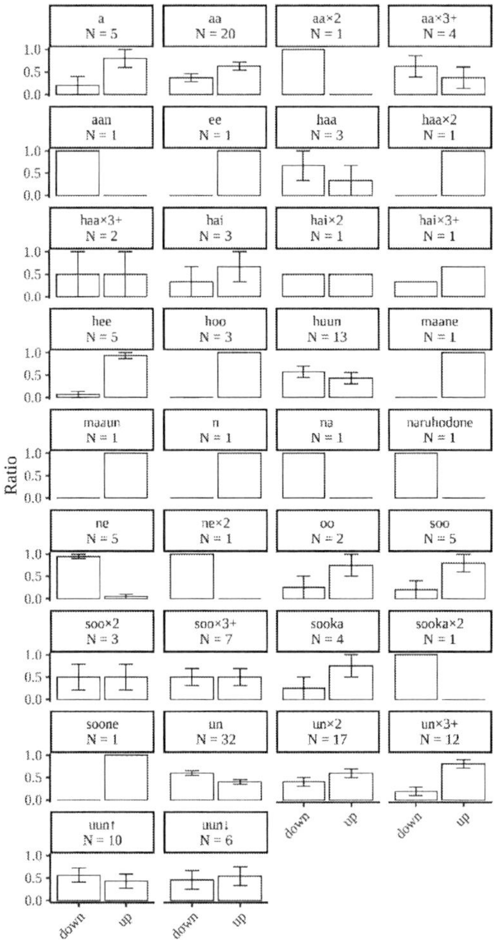

Figure 3: Ratios of up-nods and down-nods with respect to co-occurring feedback expressions

Next, we conducted statistical analysis to confirm significant difference between up-nods and down-nods. We built a generalized liner mixed model (GLMM) to predict a probability of up-nods from the feedback expressions and random intercept of participant. Since dependent variable is the binary values of up-nods and down-nods, we used Bernoulli distribution for probabilistic distribution. Parameters were estimated with Markov Chain Monte Carlo (MCMC). All these procedures were performed with R 4.2.0 (R Core Team, 2022) and the brms package 2.17.0 (Bürkner, 2017; Bürkner, 2018).

Figure 4 shows the estimated probability of up-nods with respect to co-occurring feedback expressions. Error bars show 95% confidence intervals, and expressions whose intervals do not contain 0.5 have significantly higher/lower probability of up-nods. As shown by the figure, *aa*, *ee*, *haa*×2, *hee*, *hoo*, *maane*, *maaun*, *n* and *soone* are significantly likely to co-occur with up-nods. On the other hand, *aa*×2, *aan*, *na*, *naruhodone*, *ne*, *ne*×2, *sooka*×2 and *un* are significantly likely to co-occur with down-nods.

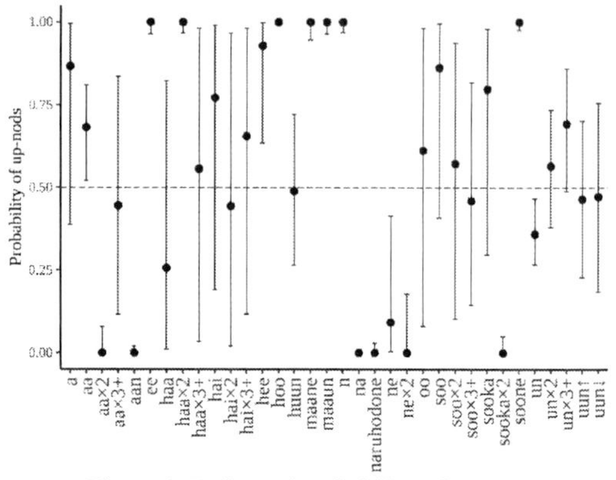

Figure 4: Estimated probability of up-nods

In conclusion, quantitative analysis showed that up-nods are used when the listener has undergone some kind of change in his or her cognitive state such as (1) when he or she receives new information (e.g., *a*, *aa*, *ee*, *hee* and *hoo*) and (2) when he or she understands preceding utterance (e.g., *un*×2 and *un*×3). On the other hand, down-nods are used (3) when he or she has prior knowledge of preceding information (e.g., *aa*, *ne*), (4) when the listener receives new but not interesting information (e.g., *huun* and *haa*) and (5) when he or she uses continuer (e.g., *un*).

4. Qualititative Analysis

4.1 Purpose

In this section, we conduct qualitative analysis of our data to presicely exmine when and how up-nods are used in terms of the type of preceding utterance.

4.2 Analysis

4.2.1 Inform

In the data, one of the positions where listeners use up-nods frequently was within or after the speaker's informing utterances. In excerpt (1), B provides the two listeners, A and C, with an information about her language skill that she can read Latin, Italian and German in line 01. This information may be new for both listeners. In addition, this informing can be heard as positive self-disclosure as well. In general, positive assessments might be more preferred as the response to this information, and in fact, A provides typical positive assesment "*sugoi* (Great)" in line 04. On the other hand, C produces only a particle "*hee* (Wow)" accompanied by an up-nod in lines 06-07, which are emotional expressions of surprise rather than assessment. This C's responses are not treated as problematic by the participants; she shows her surprise with the particle and up-nod, thereby, indirectly assessing A's skill in that it is so great that it deserves to be surprised. In fact, B repeats "*yomiageru dake da ttara* (If only reading aloud)" gazing at C in line 08, which seems to downgrade her skill; she may take A and C's assessments better than she expected. To sum up, in this case, the up-nod is used not only because the information is new, but also because of sequential preference.

(1) chiba0932 8:47-8:56
01 B: *yomu dake da ttara raten go to itaria go to*
If only reading, I can read Latin, Italian and
02 *doitsu go: wa dekiru yo*
German.
03 (0.13)
04 A: *sugoi[:*
Great.
05 B: *[hhh hu*
hhh hu
06 C: *[hee[:*
Wow.
07 [((up-nod))
08 B: *[yomiageru dake da ttara ne*
If only reading aloud.

In excerpt (2), participants talk about their angry story. Before this excerpt, C has finished his story telling, and A nominated B as next speaker and encourages him to tell his story next in line 01. However, B says he has no story to talk in line 06, and then, C pursues a new topic by proposing a "coming-of-age ceremony" story in line 10. Because A responds to it more strongly than B in lines 13-14, C misunderstands A has a story about the coming-of-age ceremony and encourages him to talk about it in line 15. However, A responds negatively in line 16, and provides an information that he did not even attend it in the first place in lines 20 and 23. After A has just said "*ore mazu i tte nai kara* (I didn't attend the coming-of-age ceremony in the first place)", C says "*a so kka* (Oh, I see)" and produces an up-nod in lines 21-22. In so doing, C seems to recognize that C's prior understanding that A attended the coming-of-age ceremony was wrong. Therefore, this information is not only new to C, but also contradicted with his prior understanding. To sum up, in this case, C's up-nod acknowledges A's new information and shows revision of his understanding at the same time.

(2) chiba0432 7:54-8:13
01 A: *tsugi Kitajima kun ((=B)) oko tta hanashi*
Next, Kitajima ((=B)), tell us your angry story.
02 C: *Wakaba-ku no hanashi*
Story about Wakaba-ku
03 (0.75)
04 B: *Wakaba-ku no hanashi*
Story about Wakaba-ku.
05 (1.08)
06 B: *iya* (0.24) *nai na toku ni*
No, nothing special.
07 C: *ji[tsu wa*
Actually
08 A: *[ue[e:[:*
Gah.
09 B: *[e [:*
Eh.
10 C: *[jitsu wa seejinshiki de [mitai na*
Like actually in the coming-of-age ceremony.
11 B: *[hara ga ta [tta*
Because I've never
12 *koto nai kara*
gotten angry.
13 A: *[aa a a*
Ah ah
14 *[aa a[a seejinshiki de [ne*
ah ah ah ah in the coming-of-age ceremony.
15 C: *[a [a [a tta a tta*
Oh. Oh. Was there? Was there?
16 A: *e nai yo hh [hu hu*
Eh, nothing. hu hu
17 C: *[na ha ha nai no ka*
na ha ha Nothing.
18 A: *iya demo* (0.05) [(0.1) *kono hito wa s-*
But this guy s-
19 B: *[ko- ika naka tta tte*
ko- He said he didn't attend.
20 A: *ore mazu i tte nai kara se[ejin shiki=*
I didn't attend the coming-of-age ceremony in the first place.
21 C: *[a so kka*
Oh, I see.
22 [((up-nod))
23 A : *=mo- moo [kae tte hen kara*
I didn't go back.
24 C : *[tooi mon na*
It's too far, isn't it?

4.2.2 Answer

The other position up-nods were frequently used was in the response to the answer to a question, especially seeking information. However, this is not surprising because we already showed that up-nods are likely to be used as acknowledgement for new information, and the answer to a question of seeking information should be new information for the questioner. In excerpt (4), C asks what club activity B did when she was a high school student in line 01. Even though the final particle "*kke*" seems to be used with consideration for the possibility she has ever heard it before, this question is designed as typical seeking information. After the question, B answers "mandolin" to this question in line 02, and then C says "*a so ka* (Oh, I see)" accompanied by an up-nod in lines 03-04. C may have heard it before and the information may not be strictly new for C, but because it is provided because of C's question, she, as the questioner, has to acknowledge it as new. Therefore, in this case, the up-nod is used not only because the information is new to C, but because C has the responsibility to acknowledge it as such as the questioner.

(3) chiba0332 1:08-1:10
01 C: *nani yatte ta [kke*
What did you do?
02 B: *[e mandori[n*
Um, mandolin.
03 C: *[a so ka*
Oh, I see,
04 [((up-nod))
05 *mandolin sa re ta n da ne*
you played the mandolin.

Before excerpt (4), B talked her story that she was suddenly asked if she could have an extra lunch box by a strange woman when she was on a train, and refused that offer. Successively, B describes the reason of her refusal that it is unclear whether or not the lunch box has already been opened in line 01. However, both A and C ask "*n*? (What?)" in lines 04-05 after a long silence of one second in line 02. Since these open class questions are typical repair initiator (Schegloff, 1977), A and C may have a trouble for B's utterance in line 01. Moreover, because the silence in line 02 is long, B also self-repairs her previous utterance by explicitly specifying the subject of the sentence as "*bento* (lunch box)" in line 03. However, this B's self-repair overlapped with A and C's repair initiations and another silence occurs in line 06. B then repairs her original utterance by rephrasing it in line 07. At its possible completion, C says "*aa aa aa aa aa aa* (Ah ah ah ah ah ah)" and simultaneously produces an up-nod in lines 08-09. In this case, although the up-nod is used as the response to an answer, like excerpt (3), it is used to show that C's trouble for the preceding utterance is resolved rather than to acknowledge a new information.

(4) chiba0832 5:26-5:35
01 B: *ai teru ka ai te nai ka mo sa yoku wakan nai jan*
It is unclear whether it is open or not, isn't it?
02 (1.03)
03 B: [*bento*
lunch box.
04 A: [*n?*
What?
05 C: [*n?*
What?
06 (0.45)
07 B: *a aa tto i kkai ake ta ka doo* [*ka*
Ah, um, whether it is open once or not.
08 C: [*aa aa aa aa aa aa*
Ah ah ah ah ah ah.
09 [((up-nod))

4.2.3 Opinion

The next position up-nods were used was in the response to an other person's opinion. Before excerpt (5), C consulted A and B about her students she teaches in part-time job and said that her students look uncomfortable when she talks about a romance in the literature class. In lines 01-03, A offers her opinion to the consultation that teachers are thought not to say such things in Japan. However, C says "*soo na no ka na* (Is that so?)" and disagrees with the A's opinion in line 04. With consideration for this C's disagreement, A adds "*watashi wa omou* (I think)" and "*baito to ka shi teru to*: (based on my experience of part-time job)" to her opinion in line 06 to downgrade the evidence of her opinion from general fact to personal experience. Moreover, A gives the exception of her opinion "very friendly students" to make more concession to C in lines 11-12 and 14-15. In response to this, C finally changes her stance and strongly agrees with A by saying "*so so so so so so soo soo* (Yeah yeah yeah yeah yeah yeah yeah yeah)" and simultaneously producing an up-nod in lines 16-18. Thus, in this case, the up-nod shows not only agreement but also the listener's change of stance form disagreement to agreement..

(5) chiba0132 1:42-2:07
01 A: *n te ka sensee ga soo yuu koto wo yuu tte yuu koto*
I mean, because teachers are thought not to say such
02 (0.343) *ga:* (1.437) *nai koto ni na tteru kara Nihon*
things like in Japan.
03 *to ka da to*
04 C: *so*[*o na no ka na*
Is that so?
05 A: [*sugoku kiki zurai n ja nai* (0.13) *to* (0.548)
It is difficult for students to ask,
06 *watashi wa omou ano* (.) *baito to ka shi teru to*[:
I think, uh, based on my experience of part-time job.
07 C: [*un*
Yeah
08 *un un*
yeah yeah.
09 (1.5)
10 C: [*mada nanka:*
Still something
11 A: [*da kara:* (0.155) *sugoi da kara* (0.227) *kudake*
So, so there are also very friendly students and
12 *ta ko mo ite:*
13 C: *u*[*n*
Yeah.
14 A: [*soo yuu ko wa nani yu tte mo* [*heeki na n da*
such students don't care whatever they are said
15 *kedo:*
and,
16 C: [*so so so so so so*
Yeah yeah yeah
17 [((up-nod))
18 *soo so*[*o*
yeah yeah yeah yeah yeah.
19 A: [*goku hutsuu no sono sensee tte yuu no wa*
there are many and very normal students
20 *sensee na n da* [*tte omoikon deru ko ga kekkoo iru*
who believe teacher is a teacher,
21 (0.149) *de sho*
aren't there?
22 C: [*un un*
Right right.
23 [((up-nod))

4.2.4 Assessment

In our data, up-nods were used as the response to assessments few times. Before excerpt (6), B told her story that she lost her train pass worth 70,000 yen when she was a high school student but her parents did not scold her. In line 01, B expresses her thought that most parents scold their children in such situation and elicits agreements form the listeners. In fact, A provides an agreement to B's thought in line 03. On the other hand, C only accepts A's thought saying "*aa* (Ah)" but does not provide an explicit agreement. The possible reason why the two listeners provide different responses to A's thought is that although agreement is preferred as a response to other person's thought in general, an agreement in this case may be heard as acknowledging A's fault, which deserves to be scolded by her parents. Because of this dilemma, C avoids providing either agreement or disagreement. Moreover, even though A once provided an agreement in line 03, she also provides an assessment "*shoo ga nai* (hopeless)" in line 07. This assessment justifies the fact that A was not scolded by her parents, and therefore, A resolves the dilemma by producing both agreement and assessment. The chage of A's stance is also shown by her use of the conjunction "*de mo* (But)" in line 07. In line 10, C strongly agrees with this assessment saying "*uu un un un u* (Yeah yeah yeah yeah yeah)" and simultaneously producing an up-nod. Even though this agreement contradicts A's thought, it can mitigate A's fault. In addition, an agreement is more preferred in this local context, i.e., after an assessment. Thus, C changes her stance from nuetral to agreement with A. To sum up, similar with excerpt (3), the up-nod shows not only agreement but also the listener's change of stance.

(6) chiba0832 7:22-7:30
01 B: *hutuu okoru yo ne:*
Most parents scold, don't they?
02 (0.60)
03 A: *so[o [ne*
Right.
04 C: *[a [a*
Ah.
05 B: *[ne*
Yeah.
06 B: *ho[nnin:*
The person
07 A: *[de mo maa shoo ga [nai kara [ne: [otoshi cha*
But well, it's hopeless, isn't it? If you lose it.
08 *ttara ne:*
08 B: *[do:no*
Which
09 A: *[ma [ho- [un*
Well ho- yeah.
10 C: *[uu un un un u*
Yeah yeah yeah yeah yeah.
[((up-nod))

4.2.5 Other

The final position up-nods were used was after the place in which the listener should respond to the speaker regardless of the type of the preceding utterance. In excerpt (7), A talks about box seats on a train in line 01 and invites listeners' responses by producing a silence in the middle of the utterance. However, because she has said only "*bokkusu* (box)" prior to the silince, its meaning is not precisely conveyed to B and C and none of them can respond to it. The design of A's utternce has changed after the silence, and an explanation of "box seats" is added in line 02, assuming the listeners do not know it. In this way, it is clear that A invites the listeners' responses during the silence and because of the lack of responses she understands they do not know "box seats". However, at the same time with A's explanation of "box seats", both B and C provide acknowledgements in lines 03-04. This sueggests that they did not understand what "box" means just after it was produced, i.e., during the silence, but have understood it by the end of line 01. B shows her noticing with a change of state token "*aa* (ah)" accompanied by a down-nod in lines 3-4. On the other hand, C responds to A with repeated "*un* (yeah)" and an up-nod in lines 05-06. Although this "*un*" can be either an answer to the A's question "*wakaru* (you know?)" or delayed response to "box", it seems that the repeated format is designed to compensate for the absence of her response during the silence. Furthermore, the repeated *un* and up-nod can be seen as an account for the absence of her timely response. That is, C also recognizes that she should have responded to A during the silence but she could not because she did not understand what "box" meant. In this way, when the listener did not respond to the speaker at the time he or she should do that, up-nods are used as a display of delayed understanding and an account for the absence of a timely response.

(7) chiba0532 0:59-1:04
01 A: *are tamani: bokkusu* (0.191) *no yatsu wakaru*
Sometimes box (0.191) ones, you know?
02 *[seki ga bokkusu n na tteru yatsu ga aru no*
There are seats built like a box.
03 B: *[aa aa aa un*
Ah ah ah yeah.
04 [((down-nod))
05 C: *[un un un aru aru aru aru*
Yeah yeah yeah there are there are there are there are.
06 [((up-nod))

4.3 Summary of the analyses

In this section, we conducted qualitative analysis and precisely examined when and how up-nods are used in Japanese conversations. First, up-nods are used to achieve multiple interactional actions. When they were used as acknowledgement for new information, they also conveyed that the listener's misunderstanding or trouble for the preceding utterance has been resolved, or that there was a sequential reason why he or she had to use them. This result suggests that the listeners might use not only verbal feedback but also up-nods at the same time in order to achieve these multiple actions. Second, up-nods are used when the listener's cognitive state has changed after hearing the preceding utterance. For instance, when up-nods were used after informing or answering, they indicate that the information provided by the utterance was not only new for the listener but contradicts his or her prior knowledge. In other case, the listener had a trouble understanding the preceding context, and used up-nods to show the preceding utterance resolved the trouble. When up-nods were used as agreement, the listener had a stance unaligned to the speaker's opinion or assessment. In these cases, the cognitive change happening inside the listener might be bigger than when the information is just new or when the listener has a similar opinion or assessment to the speaker; the possibility of using up-nods might also be higher in these cases.

5. Disscussion

In this study, we used both quantitative and qualitative analyses to investigate when and how up-nods and down-nods are used as feedback signals in Japanese conversations and how their usage differs depending on the cognitive state of the listener. As the result of the quantitative analysis, up-nods seem to co-occur with change of state feedback expressions more frequently than down-nods. This result suggests that up-nods are used when the listener did not know the information but comes to understand it by hearing the preceding utterance. On the other hand, down-nods are used with expressions indicating that the listener already knows the presented information, or the listener did not know the information but does not have interest in it, or when the listener uses a continuer. As the result of qualitative analysis, up-nods are used when the listener's cognitive state has changed after hearing the preceding utterance, for instance, if the listener had no prior knowledge about the preceding utterance, had contradicting knowledge about it or when the listener disagreed with or took a neutral stance to the speaker's opinion or assessment before the preceding utterance. Generalizing the results of the two analyses, we conclude that up-nods are related with some kind of change of cognitive state. In other words, up-nods signal cognitive change in addition to the usual meanings of nods such as "now I know it", "now I understand it" or "now I agree with it".

In this study, we can confirm that the distinction between up-nods and down-nods in Nordic cultures can be observed in Japanese. However, new question arises here; why do up-nods have similar meaning in completely distinct cultures? The most likely answer to this question is that up-nods are related with human's physiological response. This is because if up-nods had been developed from physiological response, it is natural that they are used similarly in distinct cultures. When we are surprised, we sometimes quickly move our head back. This movement may be physiological response to distance oneself from an object when we feel in danger. That is, we think up-nods are copositive movement composed of physiological head back and nods. Moreover, even though nods are used as positive feedback in many cultures, they are also used as negative, especially emotional negative feedback in Mediterranean cultures (Morris, 1977). The fact up-nods are related with the producer's emotion also supports our hypothesis.

6. Application to conversational agents

As mentioned in the beginning of the paper, in order to support natural interaction with the user, conversational agents should also have a capability to understand and generate appropriate feedback signals, and in particular, they should distinguish the different functions of up-nods and down-nods in different conversational environments. To the best of our knowledge, Wikitalk (Jokinen & Wilcock, 2014), which works in Finnish, English, and Japanese, is the first application to explicitly distinguish up-nods and down-nods as part of the Nao robot's presentation and feedback strategies. The decisions are based on a rather simple model of the robot's expectations of the continuation of the dialogue: the robot reacts to unexpected user actions, e.g., requests to stop the conversation, by up-nods signaling surprise, while it reacts to usual inform actions by down-nods.

The findings of the current study can also be applied to conversational agents: this requires that the expectation model is extended with a component that models the partner's internal cognitive state (such as knowledge, understanding and stance), and on the basis of which the agent can decide on the appropriate type of nod.

Figure 5 is a conceptual diagram of the agent with such a cognitive state update facility. First, the user produces an utterance, and the agent analyses its meaning. Second, the internal state update module calculates a new internal state and calls the feedback module. Third, the feedback module determines the type of nod depending on whether or not the internal state has been changed, and outputs the result to the gesture module. It should be noticed that although the model focuses on the type of nod to be generated, also, the type of possible verbal feedback expression is to be determined in this phase, see the CDM architecture in Jokinen & Wilcock (2014). Finally, the gesture module produces an appropriate nod, and the verbal component produces a verbal expression.

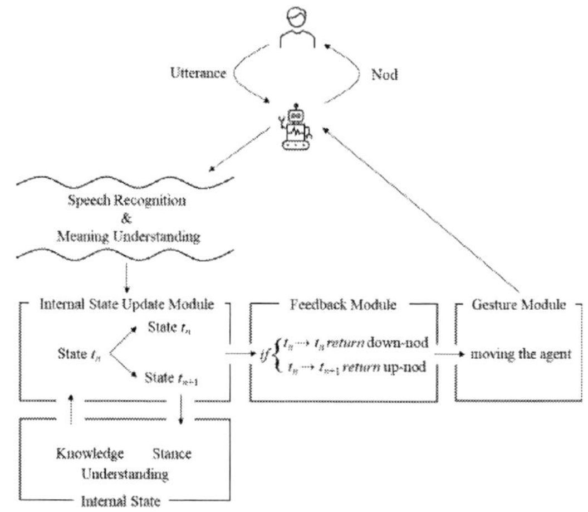

Figure 5: Conceptual diagram of the proposed system

7. Conclusion

Nods are one of the main feedback behaviors in many cultures. Moreover, this study confirmed that they are used in quit similar way in even completely distinct cultures such as Finnish and Japanese. In addition, the fact nods are important in human-human interactions suggests that they are also important in human-agent interactions. Therefore, we also proposed the architecture of the system which has the capability to generate suitable type of nod. In the future work, we aim to build a conversational agent that realizes this model and can evaluate the effectiveness of our model by subjective assessment experiment.

8. Acknowledgement

The study is based on results obtained from project JPNP20006 commissioned by the New Energy and Industrial Technology Development Organization (NEDO).

9. References

Boholm, M. & Allwood, J. (2010). Repeated head movements, their function and relation to speech. In *Proceedings of LREC 2010 Workshop on Multimodal Corpora: Advances in Capturing, Coding and Analyzing Multimodality*. Valetta, Malta.

Den, Y. & Enomoto, M. (2007). A scientific approach to conversational informatics: Description, analysis, and modeling of human conversation. In Nishida, T. (Ed.), *Conversational Informatics: An Engineering Approach*. Hoboken, NJ: John Wiley & Sons, 307-330.

Den, Y., Yoshida, N., Takanashi, K. & Koiso, H. (2011). Annotation of Japanese response tokens and preliminary analysis on their distribution in three-party conversations. In *Proceedings of the 14th Oriental COCOSDA (O-COCOSDA 2011)*, 168-173.

Endo, T. (2018). The Japanese change-of-state tokens a and aa in responsive units. *Journal of Pragmatics, 123*, 151-166.

Heritage, J. (1984). A change-of-state token and aspects of its sequential placement. In J. M. Atkinson & J. Heritage (Eds.), *Structures of Social Action*. Cambridge University Press, Cambridge, 299-345.

Jokinen, K. (2018). Dialogue models for socially intelligent robots. In Ge S. et al. (Eds.), *Social Robotics*. ICSR 2018. Lecture Notes in Computer Science, *11357*. Springer, Cham, 127-138.

Jokinen, K. & Wilcock, G. (2014). Multimodal open-domain conversations with the Nao robot. In J. Mariani, S. Rosset, M. Garnier-Rizet, & L. Devillers (Eds.), *Natural interaction with robots, knowbots and smartphones*. Springer, New York, NY, 213-224.

Kamio, A. (1994). The theory of territory of information: The case of Japanese. *Journal of Pragmatics*, *21*(1), 67-100.

Morris, D. (1977). Man watching. *A field guide to human behaviour*, Elsevier Publishing Projects Ltd., London.

Navarretta, C., Ahlsén, E., Allwood, J., Jokinen, K. & Paggio, P. (2012). Feedback in Nordic first encounters: a comparative study. In *Proceedings of LREC 2012*. Istanbul, Turkey, 2494-2499.

OpenCV. (2020). *Open Source Computer Vision Library*.

R Core Team (2022). R: The R Project for Statistical Com puting. R Foundation for Statistical Computing, Vienna, Austria. Retrieved May 20, 2022, from https://www.R-project.org/

Schegloff, E. A., Jefferson, G. & Sacks, H. (1977). The preference for self-correction in the organization of repair in conversation. *Language*, *53*(2), 361-382.

Schegloff, E. A. (1982). Discourse as an interactional achievement: some uses of "uh huh" and other things that come between sentences. In D. Tannen (Ed.), *Georgetown University Roundtable on Language and Linguistics*. Georgetown University Press, Washington, DC, 71-93.

Tanaka, H. (2010). Multimodal expressivity of the Japanese response particle huun. In D., Barth-Weingarten, E. Reber, M. Selting (Eds.), *Prosody in Interaction. John Benjamins*. Amsterdam/Philadelphia, 303-332.

Toivio, E., & Jokinen, K. (2012). Multimodal feedback si gnaling in Finnish. In A. Tavast, K. Muischnek & M. K oit (Eds.), *Human Language Technologies - The Baltics Perspective: Proceedings of the Fifth International Co nference Baltic HLT 2012 (Frontiers in Artificial Intelli gence and Applications; Vol. 247)*. IOS PRESS. 247-25 5.

Vehtari, A., Gelman, A. & Gabry, J. (2017). Practical Bayesian model evaluation using leave-one-out cross validation and WAIC, *Statistics and Computing, 27*, 1413-1432.

Vehtari, A., Gabry, J., Magnusson, M., Yao, Y., Bürkner, P., Paananen, T. & Gelman, A. (2020). loo: Efficient leave-one-out cross-validation and WAIC for Bayesian models, *R package version 2.4.1*.

Watanabe, T., Okubo, M., Nakashige, M. & Danbara, R. (2004). InterActor: Speech-driven embodied interactive actor. *International Journal of Human-Computer Interaction*, *17*(1), 43-60.

Watanabe, T. & Yuuki, N. (1989). A voice reaction system with a visualized response equivalent to nodding. *Advances in Human Factors / Ergonomics*, *12A*, 396-403.

Yatsuka, K., Kawabata, K. & Kobayashi, H. (1997). A robot listener for fluent verbal communication. *IEEE RO-MAN 7*, 408-411.

Yatsuka, K., Kawabata, K. & Kobayashi, H. (1998). A study on psychological effects of human-like interface. *IEEE RO-MAN 8*, 89-93.

Proceedings of the workshop on People in Vision, Language, and the Mind @LREC2022, pages 26–40
Marseille, 20 June 2022
© European Language Resources Association (ELRA), licensed under CC-BY-NC-4.0

Examining the Effects of Language-and-Vision Data Augmentation for Generation of Descriptions of Human Faces

Nikolai Ilinykh*, Rafal Černiavski†, Eva Elžbieta Sventickaitė†, Viktorija Buzaitė†, Simon Dobnik*
*Centre for Linguistic Theory and Studies in Probability (CLASP),
Department of Philosophy, Linguistics and Theory of Science (FLoV),
University of Gothenburg, Sweden
nikolai.ilinykh, simon.dobnik@gu.se
†Faculty of Languages, Department of Linguistics and Philology, Uppsala University, Sweden
rafal.cerniavski.2286, evaelzbieta.sventickaite.9060, viktorija.buzaite.1828@student.uu.se

Abstract

We investigate how different augmentation techniques on both textual and visual representations affect the performance of the face description generation model. Specifically, we provide the model with either original images, sketches of faces, facial composites or distorted images. In addition, on the language side, we experiment with different methods to augment the original dataset with paraphrased captions, which are semantically equivalent to the original ones, but differ in terms of their form. We also examine if augmenting the dataset with descriptions from a different domain (e.g., image captions of real-world images) has an effect on the performance of the models. We train models on different combinations of visual and linguistic features and perform both (i) automatic evaluation of generated captions and (ii) examination of how useful different visual features are for the task of facial feature classification. Our results show that although original images encode the best possible representation for the task, the model trained on sketches can still perform relatively well. We also observe that augmenting the dataset with descriptions from a different domain can boost performance of the model. We conclude that face description generation systems are more susceptible to language rather than vision data augmentation. Overall, we demonstrate that face caption generation models display a strong imbalance in the utilisation of language and vision modalities, indicating a lack of proper information fusion. We also describe ethical implications of our study and argue that future work on human face description generation should create better, more representative datasets.

Keywords: face description generation, data augmentation, feature manipulation

1. Introduction

Humans generally excel at recognising and defining everyday objects as well as human faces. However, *human face recognition* is a daily challenge to some. More than 2% of the population worldwide are affected by prosopagnosia (Corrow et al., 2016), the inability to distinguish individuals based on their facial features. As Lopatina et al. (2018) argue, the lack of the ability to recognise and describe a human face has underlying social importance, as impaired facial perception is a common indication of brain conditions, such as autism spectrum disorder. Therefore building automatic systems that can recognise human faces is essential to assist people with neurological conditions.

Although the task of face recognition has largely been solved, as state-of-the-art facial recognition models reach an accuracy of over 99% (Yan et al., 2019), the problem of **generating facial descriptions** has not received much attention. Prior research on facial cognition has shown that an attention-based model can generate captions for faces with a particular focus on emotions (Nezami et al., 2020). Similarly impressive is the performance of modern text-to-face models, which aim to generate realistic faces from short texts. Models such as the ones proposed by Nasir et al. (2019) or Sun et al. (2021) leverage powerful Generative Adversarial Networks (GANs) to produce pictures of faces that can be highly similar to natural images of faces. It has been also argued that generating facial descriptions with extra focus on words depicting emotions and sentiment is important to understand how different facial expressions can influence decision-making and inter-personal relations (Mathews et al., 2016). Nevertheless, despite these major achievements, grounding of facial features in language or generating captions of human faces remains arguably an open task, since the quality of generated descriptions remains questionable. One plausible reason is the lack of sufficient and representative data. Furthermore, features of the human face are relatively ambiguous; for instance, there is no conventional and objective measure to differentiate a small nose from a big one. Therefore we argue that it is necessary to examine both *models* and *different feature representations* for the task of automatic facial description generation, because the quality of generated texts directly affects not only the correctness of mentions of factual facial features (e.g., oval face, blond hair), but also how humans *socially* perceive and construct opinions about others in different situations and contexts (e.g., interpreting sentiment based on various facial clues).

In this paper we focus on the task of **facial description generation**. Specifically, we examine how data augmentation of either visual or linguistic representations affects performance of the face description generation model[1]. **First**, we investigate whether face captioning models demonstrate better performance when trained on various abstractions of original face images (sketches, composites, distortions). Individual features are much less pronounced in such abstractions since representations become more abstract and less specific. **Second**, we also investigate to what extent the facial captioning model can utilise visual representations and if an utterly grotesque abstraction (distorted images) affects the quality of generated captions. **Third**, we enrich the training set of facial descriptions with their counterparts, which are semantically equivalent, but differ in terms of the words and form. For example, for the description "this human has blond hair" we create the following paraphrase: "this human does not have brown hair". **Lastly**, we also evaluate the performance of statistical multi-label feature classification models trained on different visual features. With the latter, we study differences between visual abstractions and original images outside of the generation task. We conclude with a general discussion of the results and possible ethical implications of the study. We emphasise the importance of creating datasets of images of faces that would represent a more significant number of human groups and communities, while keeping in mind the right to the privacy of information.

2. Related Work

Visual Data Augmentation Data augmentation is the process of altering the dataset so as to increase the amount of data available for training. In terms of images, data augmentation usually involves rotating, flipping, resizing, and changing the colours of the images. Such a seemingly simple method often leads to considerable and consistent improvements in performance across a variety of models (Lim et al., 2019; Wang et al., 2019; Xie et al., 2020). More advanced methods of utilising data to improve the performance of models include noise reduction and image deformation. Noise reduction generally refers to the process of filtering out elements that appear to obstruct the view. For example, noise reduction is often used to eliminate Gaussian noise which can sometimes corrupt images that are being transformed (Mafi et al., 2019). Image deformation, on the other hand, is mostly used in sketch recognition and involves creating slightly changed versions of images. As formulated by Zheng et al. (2021), this method relies on learning temporal patterns in drawing a sketch and using them to deform the sketch. Having more sketches created through augmentations boosts performance sketch recognition models. Deformation can also be applied to images by performing domain adaptation (Wang et al., 2020). If the target domain involves abstraction, this method can be thought of as incorporating both noise reduction and image deformation, since the output of such a model is, for instance, a sketch which discards any non-essential information. It should be noted that, unlike pictures or images, sketches are often limited to just a few lines or strokes on white background. Thus, models are required to perform recognition from fewer features.

Language Data Augmentation Different methods are typically used to caption an image (Bernardi et al., 2017): from templates (Fang et al., 2015) to end-to-end systems (Kiros et al., 2014) with attention (Wang et al., 2016; Xu et al., 2015; Lu et al., 2017). More recently, a transformer architecture has been adopted for many multi-modal tasks including image captioning[2]. Augmenting datasets with additional captions incorporating certain linguistic variation has been shown to improve performance of captioning models. Zhang et al. (2015) replace words with synonyms based on the thesaurus from WordNet (Fellbaum, 2005), whereas Fadaee et al. (2017) propose an augmentation method for a machine translation model which targets rare words. Kobayashi (2018) implements contextual augmentation for convolutional and recurrent neural networks. In general, researchers use deletion, insertion, replacement or swap techniques at either character or word level to augment captions (Zhang et al., 2015).

3. Augmenting the Task Dataset

Motivation It is not immediately clear how to augment data for models that operate with multiple modalities. The key challenge is to change representations for both modalities in such a way that these changes are relatively comparable and have similar conceptual motivation behind. In general, data augmentation either adds or removes specific features. Such strategies allow for better understanding of how and what models learn. In terms of *visual augmentation*, we constructed different abstract representations (sketches) of images of faces. When generating sketches, we simultaneously *reduce* individual visual features (e.g., abstract sketches look much more similar to each other versus images of faces, which are more varied in terms of individual features) and bring abstract representations to the fore, *introducing* input representations to the captioning model which are more distilled (e.g., general facial features on sketches are more pronounced). In terms of *textual augmentation*, we *add* features by generating alternative descriptions of images, which introduce new vocabulary items to learn for the model. By generating such alternative texts, we also *exclude* direct correspondence of descriptions into images of faces and make grounding task for the model much harder, because generated descriptions of faces do not use the exact same words as the ground truth description. Overall, we believe that our augmentation methods introduce comparable conditions for both language

[1]Our work is an examination of whether vision-and-language model relies on biases in feature representations or learns spurious correlations (Agarwal et al., 2020).

[2]For an overview of many different architectures, we refer the reader to Bugliarello et al. (2021).

and vision, in which different types of information are either removed or added.

Face Description Dataset We use *CelebA-HQ* dataset (Karras et al., 2017) as our task dataset for training and testing facial description generation models. The dataset contains $30,000$ high-resolution images of human faces of celebrities with 10 natural language descriptions per each image. On average, each description is 15.53 tokens long, e.g., Figure 3. The dataset also provides binary annotations of 40 facial features. The size of the training set in all experiments is set to the first E entries from the dataset ($E = 10,000$).

Augmenting Vision Zhang et al. (2011) have shown that the human recognition rate of facial sketches is largely affected by the sketch quality and the level of detail. This finding indicates that image manipulation should be conducted very carefully: the face has to be still recognisable while its representation can become highly abstract, e.g. containing contours of some parts of faces. Therefore, we control the level of abstraction by generating *three* different sketches per image.

First, we run a simple auto-encoder architecture (Rumelhart et al., 1986) to transform images into sketches.[3] This is an unsupervised neural network which consists of an encoder that compresses data into vectors and passes them through multiple convolutional layers (Cun et al., 1990). Next, a decoder learns to reconstruct the original data as closely as possible from these vectors. Backpropagation is used to minimise the reconstruction loss. We train the model for 100 epochs with the Adam optimiser (Kingma and Ba, 2014). We further refer to this type of sketches as **Face-2-Sketch**.

Second, we follow Zhu et al. (2017) and implement a generative adversarial network for image-to-image translation task. This model is a combination of two networks, a generator and a discriminator, which use two unaligned sets of images, A and B, to identify their similarities and transform images from the first set of images to images of the second set. The model is using the cycle consistency loss expressed as follows:

$$\begin{aligned} \boldsymbol{L}(\mathbf{G}, \mathbf{F}, \mathbf{D}_A, \mathbf{D}_B) = \quad & \boldsymbol{L}_{GAN}(\mathbf{G}, \mathbf{D}_A, \mathbf{A}, \mathbf{B}) + \\ & \boldsymbol{L}_{GAN}(\mathbf{F}, \mathbf{D}_B, \mathbf{B}, \mathbf{A}) + , \\ & \lambda \boldsymbol{L}_{CYC}(\mathbf{G}, \mathbf{F}) \end{aligned} \quad (1)$$

where $\mathbf{G}$ and $\mathbf{F}$ are mappings from image set $\mathbf{A}$ to $\mathbf{B}$ and vice versa, $\mathbf{D}_A$ and $\mathbf{D}_B$ are discriminators that are trained to differentiate between real and predicted images, and λ parameter controls the contribution of each loss for the final loss score. We achieve the best performance loss-wise with the GAN model after 5 epochs of training. We also train the model for 33 epochs in total to see the extent to which the model can over-fit and generate distorted, grotesque sketches. The resulting sketches might be highly dissimilar to the original images and we use them to investigate whether our facial description generator could still learn from highly unrecognizeable images. We thus use both models which we refer to as **GAN:Composite** and **GAN:Distorted** respectively. We set $\lambda = 10$, the learning rate $l = 0.0002$, batch size $b = 1$ and a weight decay $wd = 0.00001$ after each epoch.

Both **Face-2-Sketch** and **GAN** models were trained on the combination of three datasets: CUHK dataset (Wang and Tang, 2009a) consisting of 188 face-sketch pairs, AR dataset (Martinez and Benavente, 1998) with 123 photo-sketch pairs, and CUHK Face Sketch FERET Database (CUFSF) (Wang and Tang, 2009b; Zhang et al., 2011) of 1,194 sketches, for which we additionally obtained the FERET (Phillips et al., 1998) database with pictures of 1,194 people. We resize the pictures and sketches to 200×250. In addition, since FERET dataset contains pictures from various angles, we manually cleaned the dataset, leaving only one profile picture per person. Examples of the images received with different visual augmentation methods are shown in Figure 1, check Figure 4 for more examples.

Augmenting Language Kafle et al. (2017) use two methods for data augmentation for Visual Question Answering on real-world images: (i) template-based generation of texts based on rich object annotations of images and (ii) LSTMs (Hochreiter and Schmidhuber, 1997) to generate texts that resemble structure of the original texts. While images in captioning datasets such as MSCOCO (Lin et al., 2014) include a large variety of objects, images of faces are much more rigid in terms of observable parts: nose, mouth, etc. Parts of the face can differ on the level of attributes (shape, flatness, openness, for example) and a simple method to augment our dataset with more descriptions of each face is to *generate new sentences by changing verbs, adjectives and adverbs* which typically depict attributes.

In our search for the most suitable method for language augmentation we decided to examine an existing tool, the `nlpaug`[4] library. This library allows us to try a variety of existing language models and use different word embedding representations extracted by feeding captions to such models as word2vec(Mikolov et al., 2013), GloVe(Pennington et al., 2014), FastText(Mikolov et al., 2018), BERT(Devlin et al., 2019), DistilBERT(Sanh et al., 2019), and RoBERTA(Zhuang et al., 2021). Based on the similarity of extracted embeddings, `nlpaug` either (i) substitutes words in captions with synonyms or (ii) inserts additional words inside captions. In addition, this library allows us to use WordNet hierarchies from the nltk library (Bird et al., 2009) in order to manipulate with the original descriptions, replacing words with either synonyms or antonyms. Examples of the captions obtained with dif-

[3]We adapt the code from `https://www.kaggle.com/theblackmamba31/photo-to-sketch-using-autoencoder/notebook`.

[4]`https://github.com/makcedward/nlpaug`

Figure 1: Example of the image from the task dataset. We show original, composite, sketch-based and distorted images in order from the most left one to the right.
Ground truth description: This person is attractive, and young and has bags under eyes, wavy hair, arched eyebrows, and mouth slightly open.
Feature annotations: Arched_Eyebrows, Attractive, Bags_Under_Eyes, Blond_Hair, Heavy_Makeup, High_Cheekbones, Mouth_Slightly_Open, No_Beard, Smiling, Wavy_Hair, Wearing_Earrings, Wearing_Lipstick, Wearing_Necklace, Young.
Augmented description: This person is not unattractive, and not old and doesn't have flat under eyes, straight hair, straight eyebrows, and mouth completely closed.

ferent `nlpaug` methods and the ground truth facial description are shown in Table 2. During manual examination of resulting descriptions, we noticed that the augmented captions were in most cases incorrect: they neither followed the proper English grammar nor they referred to the features present or absent in the picture.[5] To make sure that augmented captions do not contradict with images, we developed *a rule-based algorithm* that replaces all verbs, adjectives, and adverbs (a set of 28 word types in total) with antonyms. The list of words to be replaced was designed manually by two authors of the paper. Different replacements were agreed through discussion; the whole list is shown in Table 3. First, we carefully selected antonyms from thesauri and dictionaries so as to ensure that the antonyms refer to what is considered *the opposite of facial features*, e.g. round face → square face; blond hair → black hair. Next, we negated each antonym, e.g. square face → not square face; black hair → not black hair. Example of the resulting description and ground truth text are shown in Table 2, in which we can see that both augmented caption and ground truth description correspond to each other due to the mention of the same feature but in a different way, e.g. "is attractive" and "is not unattractive", "young" and "not old". Note that the experiments that we report in this paper were conducted *only* with captions generated with our rule-based algorithm and list of the words to be replaced; we did not use any `nlpgaug`-based methods for our experiments due to bad quality of augmented captions.
We note that replacing verbs, adjectives and adverbs with their antonyms or negated counterparts *guaranteed* that the negative captions were still semantically correct, since the generated captions addressed the features that the faces lacked rather than possessed, e.g. the person has wavy hair → the person does not have straight hair. We believe it is important to see whether the models will be able to pick up an important linguistic cue - negation - and tailor its output accordingly (Niu and Bansal, 2018). Our method of data augmentation also enforces the model to learn to reason with language (e.g., wavy hair is not straight hair), which could potentially improve the quality of feature grounding between language and vision. At the same time, the vocabulary of the model is increased because of the introduction of antonyms which make language modality more prominent as a feature. Note that the combination of antonyms and negated relations ("with" → "without") creates ambiguity and therefore such descriptions are harder to learn: "hat" can be identified by visual features but it is unclear what visual features "without a hat" can be identified with. Overall, due to language augmentation the task becomes much harder and we expect that this will be reflected in the performance.

Manual Evaluation of Augmentation Examples from each of the four sets of images can be seen in Figure 4. The quality of the sketches differs greatly across all models: sketches of white women, who constituted nearly half of the dataset, were most accurate, whereas sketches of other people were more distorted overall. We believe that to the naked eye, **GAN:Composite** were the most successful in terms of condensing the facial features. When it comes to the **Face2Sketch** subset, the quality was considerably poorer. Nevertheless, some of the features are still visible. Images in the **GAN:Distorted** subset appeared to have additional noise that partially masks some of the facial features. Examples of augmented captions are shown in Table 2 describing features of the original image in Figure 1.

[5] Interestingly, our manual examination also indirectly evaluated augmentation methods introduced in `nlpaug`, showing that these methods have many flaws.

4. Facial Description Generation

Model Our face description generator is a simple CNN-LSTM encoder-decoder network with attention (Xu et al., 2015)[6]. The model is trained with cross-entropy loss as well as doubly stochastic regularisation. We pick the best checkpoint based on the BLEU score (Papineni et al., 2002) on the validation set and do early stopping. We train the model for 20 epochs and set the batch size to $b = 5$, learning rate to $lr = 1e - 4$ for the encoder and $lr = 4e - 4$ for the decoder, dropout to $d = 0.5$ and gradient clipping $gc = 5$.

Training and Evaluation The description generation model is trained on either original images (**Baseline**) or on one of the three types of visual manipulations (**GAN:Composite**, **GAN:Distorted**, **Face-2-Sketch**). We add `start` and `end` to the captions and pad shorter descriptions. We use 5 captions per image for training. As the vocabulary of the descriptions is rather limited, we manipulate training data by augmenting the captions with a mix of original and generated descriptions with a ratio of 3:2 (3 original and 2 augmented captions) and name this condition **Aug-Anton 3:2**. We also replace all five descriptions per image with augmented ones for **Aug-Anton 5**. In addition, we augment training data by injecting the model with a small portion of the caption from *Flickr8k* dataset (Hodosh et al., 2013): we add 12.5% in training and validation sets which corresponds to 1000 and 125 of image-caption pairs respectively (both images and captions were added to the our task dataset). The latter model is referred to as **Aug-Caption**. The vocabulary expanded to 100 when data with antonyms was produced and to 470 when a variant with image captions is used. We evaluate the models on three types of data: (i) the original images, (ii) the composites produced by **GAN:Composite**, and (iii) distorted images from **GAN:Distorted**. By running our models on different evaluation sets we aim to measure whether the distillation of features has a desirable effect on captions.

Results We report BLEU-1 (Papineni et al., 2002), METEOR (Banerjee and Lavie, 2005) and ROUGE (Lin, 2004) scores for generated captions. Table 1 shows the results of automatic evaluation of generated face descriptions and Figure 2 shows examples of descriptions generated with different vision and language augmentation methods. Red-coloured values indicate best models among those, which were trained with original, composites, sketches or distorted images, e.g. visual augmentation. Blue-coloured values depict best models among those which were trained on a dataset in which we augmented only the textual side (original images were used for training). We note that in our evaluation of linguistically augmented models we compared generated texts against their non-augmented counterparts. For example, while the **Aug-Anton 3:2** model has been trained on both "tall" and "not short" in respective captions, it has been evaluated only against the one that has "tall" in it. With this harsh evaluation we aimed to see whether models learn more distinct representations for target words ("tall") when trying to contrast them with their negated antonyms.

METEOR	**1. img**	**2. cmp**	**3. dst**
A. Baseline	72.87	60.27	60.35
B. GAN:Composite	59.47	72.76	66.95
C. Face-2-Sketch	72.87	61.86	61.36
D. GAN:Distorted	57.17	64.22	70.93
E. Aug-Caption	69.98	39.06	46.03
F. Aug-Anton 3:2	**72.51**	**62.34**	**61.29**
G. Aug-Anton 5	41.02	32.71	33.35
BLEU-1	**1. img**	**2. cmp**	**3. dst**
A. Baseline	48.12	30.41	29.18
B. GAN:Composite	26.84	43.76	33.71
C. Face-2-Sketch	39.91	24.22	25.39
D. GAN:Distorted	27.75	36.29	43.69
E. Aug-Caption	**49.71**	12.94	17.79
F. Aug-Anton 3:2	39.09	**30.65**	**32.41**
G. Aug-Anton 5	13.84	7.10	8.71
ROUGE	**1. img**	**2. cmp**	**3. dst**
A. Baseline	64.36	53.13	54.41
B. GAN:Composite	54.36	62.07	57.67
C. Face-2-Sketch	59.58	50.11	51.19
D. GAN:Distorted	53.27	62.07	62.65
E. Aug-Caption	**65.81**	44.41	48.03
F. Aug-Anton 3:2	59.46	**54.31**	**54.08**
G. Aug-Anton 5	42.33	35.52	35.76

Table 1: Automatic evaluation of generated facial descriptions. We report results for three NLG metrics: METEOR, BLEU-1 and ROUGE split into three tables. In each table each row depicts a type of the (non-)augmented data that the model has been trained on. The first set of models include those which were trained on either original dataset (*Baseline*) or visual augmentations (captions were kept untouched). The second set of models below a dashed line shows models trained with different language augmentations but with original images. The columns show the type of data each model has been evaluated on: *img* stands for original images, *cmp* and *dst* are for composites and distorted images respectively.

We first analyse the performance of the models which were trained with *visual* augmentations (B - D). The **Baseline** model, which is trained on original images, performs best when tested on original images, which is expected. Notably, **Face-2-Sketch** that is trained on facial sketches achieves the same METEOR score and is also the second best in terms of BLEU and ROUGE scores when tested on original images. This indicates that our model either (i) cannot fully use original visual representations and this is why its performance is close to the model trained on sketches or (ii) the model is actually able to sufficiently learn from sketches of faces.

[6]We use the code from `https://github.com/sgrvinod/a-PyTorch-Tutorial-to-Image-Captioning`.

When tested on composite and distorted images, the best models are the ones that were trained on the corresponding visual augmentations. As expected the **Baseline** model suffers the most when tested on non-original images. Interestingly, the **Face-2-Sketch** model shows one of the worst performances when tested on composites and distorted images, while it is on par with the baseline when tested on original images. The result implies that only a particular level of abstraction of faces is exploited by the model to generate better descriptions: a simple auto-encoder, although producing very abstract representations, outperforms the generative adversarial network which likely generates sketches with high contrast, high level of details and high distortions as shown by the examples in Figure 4. We conclude that it is important to consider the network type and abstractness of its output when performing visual augmentation of multi-modal datasets.

The bottom parts of the table below the dashed lines show performance of the models augmented with different *linguistic* representations (E - G). For two out of three metrics, the model that has been jointly trained on both facial descriptions and image captions (**Aug-Caption**) performs best when tested on original images. Partial augmentation with descriptions with the same meaning but different form (**Aug-Anton 3:2**) leads to the second-best performance with the exception of the METEOR metric where this model performs best. This can be attributed to the fact that METEOR is designed specifically for better synonym matching and linking of paraphrased sentences and therefore its high score indirectly reflects that our method of mixing original descriptions with paraphrased descriptions (training for **Aug-Anton 3:2**) is helpful for the model. In contrast, using only augmented descriptions results in a drop in performance, possibly because the model is not able to learn grounding of descriptions in visual features. The model is required to perform extra reasoning to ground augmented descriptions since they correspond to a variety of visual features. It has been shown that METEOR generally correlates better with human judgements unlike BLEU or ROUGE (Elliott and Keller, 2014) which means augmenting facial descriptions with our simple method can generate more human-like descriptions. When tested on *composite* and *distorted* images, **Aug-Anton 3:2** performs best across all metrics. Interestingly, in terms of BLEU, **Aug-Caption** and **Aug-Anton 5** show a much lower performance than **Aug-Anton 3:2** when tested on both composite and distorted images. It is possible that when visual features are very different from what the model has been trained on (trained on original images, but tested on composites and distorted), the model starts relying on fine-grained differences in linguistic augmented descriptions which also introduce contrast in form but not in meaning. At the same time, training the model on augmented descriptions only (**Aug-Anton 5**) results in a very low performance in terms of BLEU (7.10 and 8.71 for composites and distorted respectively), because the model does not have access to a suitable representation in either of the modalities. Also, the fact that models F and G were evaluated against untouched captions might lead to generally lower metric results compared to model E.
Overall, note that **Aug-Caption** has shown a relatively good performance in terms of all testing conditions for METEOR and ROUGE. When we test this model (model E in Table 1) on original images, straightforward replacement of words (models F and G) does not bring better learning, but using captions from a different domain does. This is because captions from a different domain introduce a larger variety of syntactic structures and semantic relations between words in text. In comparison, our manual linguistic augmentation does not change either syntax or semantics of descriptions - it simply introduces new words into the vocabulary. At the same time, the model which learns to discriminate between descriptions which are identical in terms of their meaning but different in terms of their form (model F) achieves higher scores across multiple conditions and metrics. Therefore we conclude that augmenting language has a positive effect on the model's performance when (i) there is a strong form-based contrasting signal from descriptions like in **Aug-Anton 3:2** model, and (ii) the data is infused with descriptions from a similar multi-modal domain (**Aug-Caption**), e.g. image captioning. We also believe that future work should examine the extent of how much does the face description generation model benefit from being trained on captions from different multi-modal domains and tasks.

5. Multi-Label Feature Classification

In addition to caption generation we also evaluate the augmented visual datasets on another task, facial feature classification.

Model We train two statistical classifiers: Random Forest and k-Nearest Neighbours. We use the annotations of K features for every image provided by the authors of the dataset. Each classifier takes a feature vector of the image as its input $v_n \in \mathbf{R}^{1 \times D}$, where $D = 2048$, and learns to predict one of the K feature annotations, $K = 40$. Examples of the feature annotation are shown in Figure 4. Note that most of these features could overlap with the vocabulary of the image captioning model, but some of them are also more abstract, e.g. *5_o_Clock_Shadow*. *Blurry*. We aim to examine the effect of different visual representations on the performance of the classification model.

Training and evaluation We use a randomly selected sample of 9,000 images as a training set and another 1,000 as the test set to train and evaluate all models on the *CelebA-HQ* dataset. We use loss as the objective function and other standard parameters with the scikit-learn API (Pedregosa et al., 2011). The performance of the multi-label linear classification mod-

Original description:
The person has big lips, sideburns, goatee, mustache, and brown hair. He is wearing necktie.

Evaluated on original images:
Baseline: the man has sideburns and wears necktie
GAN:Composite: this man has big lips and black hair and is wearing hat
GAN:Distorted: this person has bags under eyes and is wearing lipstick
Face-2-Sketch: the man has bags under eyes and big nose
Aug-Caption: the person is young and has big nose and bags under eyes
Aug-Anton 3:2: this person has bags under eyes and big nose
Aug-Anton 5: this man differ old and refuse bags under eyes and little nose

Evaluated on composites:
Baseline: this man has big nose and big lips
GAN:Composite: this person has bags under eyes and big nose and is wearing necktie
GAN:Distorted: this woman has big nose and is wearing lipstick and hat
Face-2-Sketch: the man has big nose and bags under eyes
Aug-Caption: the person is chubby and has goatee and big nose
Aug-Anton 3:2: the person has bags under eyes and big lips
Aug-Anton 5: the person differ old and refuse pale skin and white hair

Evaluated on distorted images:
Baseline: the woman has big lips and wears lipstick and earrings
GAN:Composite: this person has big lips and is wearing hat
GAN:Composite: this person has bags under eyes big nose and sideburns
Face-2-Sketch: the person has big lips and wears lipstick
Aug-Caption: the person has gray hair and big nose and is wearing necklace
Aug-Anton 3:2: the person has mouth slightly open and big lips *Aug-Anton 5:* the person differ smiling and refuse mouth slightly closed bags under eyes and low cheekbones

Figure 2: Example of an image with the original description and texts generated by our models described in Table 1.

els was evaluated with reference to both the micro and macro averages of precision, recall, and F-score. We gave equal weight to precision and recall in calculating the F-score.

Results The results are shown in Figure 5. In terms of the F1-score, we do not observe any noticeable differences between performances of different features across both micro- and macro-averaged results. The same holds for the results on recall metric. Most notably, both k-NN and Random Forest model have the highest macro-average precision and recall on **Face-2-Sketch** features, which, we argue, is the least informative of the facial features. As can be seen from the graphs, macro-averaging is generally in a lower range than micro-averaging, demonstrating that model's performance on the non-majority classes is worse than on the majority classes. This result reflects that the model can mostly predict some of the most frequent facial features, which are often represented in the dataset (such as *female* and *attractive*), yet fail to predict rare features, such as *goatee* and *receding_hairline*. We leave a deeper investigation of the effect that the dataset imbalance has on the performance of the model on the feature classification task for future work.

Overall, visual features seem to be very similar with each other since using them interchangeably with each other does not affect the results on the feature classification task. High similarity of different visual features can also be one of the reasons why different models for visual augmentations (A-D in Table 1) do not differ so much from each other in terms of different evaluation metrics. In comparison, language augmentation methods (E-G) can affect performance of the model to a larger extent, e.g. **Aug-Anton 5** decreasing the overall performance to BLEU of 13.84 on the original images. Therefore we argue that the model is much more sensitive to language augmentation possibly because visual representations are very similar to each other and are not distinctive enough as the results on feature classification task demonstrate. This indirectly supports the idea that multi-modal architectures strongly learn to benefit from the language modality instead of visual representations whatsoever because language is more informative and mostly harder to predict (Frank et al., 2021).

6. General Discussion

Automatic evaluation of facial descriptions has revealed that, first and foremost, the original photos are generally better suited for the task. This may be due to the fact that both **Baseline** and **Aug-Caption** receive fully-coloured images as input, whereas other conditions such as **GAN:Composite**, **GAN:Distorted** and **Face-2-Sketch** are trained on gray-scale generated images distributed over 3 colour channels. This indicates that using sketches or other abstract representations of faces does not necessarily improve the quality of generated descriptions. In addition, as can be seen from Figure4, the images obtained with **Face-2-Sketch** are the most abstract ones. Nonetheless, automatic evaluation metrics for models trained on this data are higher compared to **GAN:Composite** and **GAN:Distorted**. As such, the reason for these differences could be that during the pooling process the features are meshed in such a manner that the high-quality of images may not be necessary for rather adequate performance. Finally, introducing only antonyms without mixing them with original descriptions results in incorrect or impossible grounding of visual features with descriptions which are not encoded by those visual features. It is important to introduce both correct descriptions and their augmented versions so that the model learns from both texts, which are semantically equivalent but differ in terms of their form.

6.1. Ethical Implications

The current study touches upon ethical implications of representation ability in data used for computer vision and natural language processing tasks. We note that our task dataset, *CelebA-HQ*, is over-represented with high-quality images of humans of specific race, gender and ethnicity. This potentially leads to considerable bias in models, since the models are predominantly exposed to a very limited groups since most datasets include Caucasian and Asian people. Ensuring that a bigger number of groups are represented in the dataset is costly and difficult. Alternative ways of debiasing and exposing models to more diverse set of images of faces are highly needed. At the same time, what matters is the correctness and fairness of face descriptions: they should depict only concrete face features without any subjective, sensitive or offensive descriptions.

The language augmentation approach proposed in this paper is an attempt at exposing the models to features that are not present in the dataset and thus compensate for the lack of representation of images through linguistic knowledge. For instance, it is challenging or even counterproductive to generate synthetic faces with various features that are not represented in the dataset. On the other hand, generating augmented descriptions with semantically similar words is a relatively simple yet effective way towards exposing the model to features that are not present in the data, yet possible. We acknowledge that our simple approach is without a doubt insufficient for ensuring a better coverage of different groups of people, as human features, unlike synonymity-antonymity, are non-binary: the colour of hair can be blond, black, brunette, whichever other colour, or there could be no hair at all. Nevertheless, we believe that future work should focus on the language augmentation method of face description datasets with the emphasis on creating semantically correct, but also diverse descriptions.

7. Conclusion and Future Work

In this project, we aimed to investigate the effects of visual and linguistic augmentation as means of improving automatic generation of facial descriptions. In particular, we operated with different levels of visual abstractions and paraphrases of descriptions and tracked how these modifications alter the generated texts. We also investigated how different visual representations affected the feature classification with linear models. Our results show that original images are generally more useful for the facial description generation task. However, different feature manipulation have a different effect on the resulting texts: augmenting linguistic representations in a contrasting way (keeping original descriptions and adding artificially created ones) has a larger effect on model's learning ability unlike augmenting data from the vision side. For the latter, using auto-encoded sketch-like features of faces is generally more preferable rather than using facial composites, possibly due to the level of abstractness of sketches. Also, we have shown that linguistic augmentation of the dataset with captions from a different domain could lead to better face descriptions.

In terms of future work, we suggest the following experiments: in terms of visual augmentation, first, manipulate the model in such a manner that it could accommodate training on different types of visual data in parallel. One approach may be to experiment with different combinations of sets of images, composites, and distorted pictures through dense layers and examine how it would affect the captions. Furthermore, the images could be manipulated to limit one or more colour channels at a time, thus, more information could be extracted on how the colouring of the images affects the training and, in turn, the attention and quality of the generated captions. In terms of language augmentation, we propose to run the experiments in parallel with data in multiple languages to assess whether features that are mapped to certain tokens in different languages are the same, e.g. feature grounding task.

8. Acknowledgements

NI and SD were supported by a grant from the Swedish Research Council (VR project 2014-39) for the establishment of the Centre for Linguistic Theory and Studies in Probability (CLASP) at the University of Gothenburg.

9. Bibliographical References

Agarwal, V., Shetty, R., and Fritz, M. (2020). Towards causal vqa: Revealing and reducing spurious correlations by invariant and covariant semantic editing. In *IEEE/CVF Conference on Computer Vision and Pattern Recognition (CVPR)*, pages 9690–9698, June.

Atliha, V. and Šešok, D. (2020). Text Augmentation Using BERT for Image Captioning. *Applied Sciences*, 10:5978.

Banerjee, S. and Lavie, A. (2005). Meteor: An automatic metric for mt evaluation with improved correlation with human judgments. In *Proceedings of the acl workshop on intrinsic and extrinsic evaluation measures for machine translation and/or summarization*, pages 65–72.

Bernardi, R., Cakici, R., Elliott, D., Erdem, A., Erdem, E., Ikizler-Cinbis, N., Keller, F., Muscat, A., and Plank, B. (2017). Automatic description generation from images: A survey of models, datasets, and evaluation measures (extended abstract). In *Proceedings of the Twenty-Sixth International Joint Conference on Artificial Intelligence, IJCAI-17*, pages 4970–4974.

Bird, S., Klein, E., and Loper, E. (2009). *Natural language processing with Python*. O'Reilly.

Bugliarello, E., Cotterell, R., Okazaki, N., and Elliott, D. (2021). Multimodal pretraining unmasked: A meta-analysis and a unified framework of vision-and-language BERTs. *Transactions of the Association for Computational Linguistics*, 9:978–994.

Cornia, M., Stefanini, M., Baraldi, L., and Cucchiara, R. (2020). Meshed-memory transformer for image captioning. In *Proceedings of the IEEE/CVF Conference on Computer Vision and Pattern Recognition*, pages 10578–10587.

Corrow, S. L., Dalrymple, K. A., and Barton, J. J. (2016). Prosopagnosia: current perspectives. *Eye and brain*, 8:165.

Cun, Y. L., Boser, B., Denker, J. S., Howard, R. E., Habbard, W., Jackel, L. D., and Henderson, D., (1990). *Handwritten Digit Recognition with a Back-Propagation Network*, page 396–404. Morgan Kaufmann Publishers Inc., San Francisco, CA, USA.

Devlin, J., Chang, M.-W., Lee, K., and Toutanova, K. (2019). BERT: Pre-training of deep bidirectional transformers for language understanding. In *Proceedings of the 2019 Conference of the North American Chapter of the Association for Computational Linguistics: Human Language Technologies, Volume 1 (Long and Short Papers)*, pages 4171–4186, Minneapolis, Minnesota.

Dosovitskiy, A., Beyer, L., Kolesnikov, A., Weissenborn, D., Zhai, X., Unterthiner, T., Dehghani, M., Minderer, M., Heigold, G., Gelly, S., et al. (2020). An image is worth 16x16 words: Transformers for image recognition at scale. *arXiv preprint arXiv:2010.11929*.

Duchaine, B. (2011). Developmental prosopagnosia: Cognitive, neural, and developmental investigations. In Andy Calder, et al., editors, *Oxford Handbook of Face Perception*, pages 821–838. Oxford University Press.

Elliott, D. and Keller, F. (2014). Comparing automatic evaluation measures for image description. In *Proceedings of the 52nd Annual Meeting of the Association for Computational Linguistics (Volume 2: Short Papers)*, pages 452–457, Baltimore, Maryland, June. Association for Computational Linguistics.

Fadaee, M., Bisazza, A., and Monz, C. (2017). Data Augmentation for Low-Resource Neural Machine Translation. *ArXiv*, abs/1705.00440.

Fang, H., Gupta, S., Iandola, F., Srivastava, R. K., Deng, L., Dollár, P., Gao, J., He, X., Mitchell, M., Platt, J. C., et al. (2015). From captions to visual concepts and back. In *Proceedings of the IEEE conference on computer vision and pattern recognition*, pages 1473–1482.

Fellbaum, C. (2005). Wordnet and wordnets. In Keith Brown, editor, *Encyclopedia of Language and Linguistics*, pages 665–670, Oxford. Elsevier.

Frank, S., Bugliarello, E., and Elliott, D. (2021). Vision-and-language or vision-for-language? on cross-modal influence in multimodal transformers. In *Proceedings of the 2021 Conference on Empirical Methods in Natural Language Processing*, pages 9847–9857, Online and Punta Cana, Dominican Republic, November. Association for Computational Linguistics.

Hochreiter, S. and Schmidhuber, J. (1997). Long short-term memory. *Neural computation*, 9(8):1735–1780.

Kafle, K., Yousefhussien, M., and Kanan, C. (2017). Data augmentation for visual question answering. In *Proceedings of the 10th International Conference on Natural Language Generation*, pages 198–202, Santiago de Compostela, Spain, September. Association for Computational Linguistics.

Kingma, D. P. and Ba, J. (2014). Adam: A method for stochastic optimization. cite arxiv:1412.6980Comment: Published as a conference paper at the 3rd International Conference for Learning Representations, San Diego, 2015.

Kiros, R., Salakhutdinov, R., and Zemel, R. (2014). Multimodal neural language models. In *International conference on machine learning*, pages 595–603. PMLR.

Kobayashi, S. (2018). Contextual Augmentation: Data Augmentation by Words with Paradigmatic Relations. *ArXiv*, abs/1805.06201.

Li, J., Yu, X., Peng, C., and Wang, N. (2017). Adaptive representation-based face sketch-photo synthesis. *Neurocomputing*, 269:152–159.

Li, X., Yin, X., Li, C., Hu, X., Zhang, P., Zhang, L., Wang, L., Hu, H., Dong, L., Wei, F., Choi, Y., and Gao, J. (2020). Oscar: Object-semantics aligned pre-training for vision-language tasks. *ECCV 2020*.

Lim, S., Kim, I., Kim, T., Kim, C., and Kim, S. (2019). Fast autoaugment. In *NeurIPS*.

Lin, T.-Y., Maire, M., Belongie, S., Bourdev, L., Girshick, R., Hays, J., Perona, P., Ramanan, D., Zitnick, C. L., and Dollár, P. (2014). Microsoft coco: Common objects in context. cite arxiv:1405.0312Comment: 1) updated annotation pipeline description and figures; 2) added new section describing datasets splits; 3) updated author list.

Lin, C.-Y. (2004). Rouge: A package for automatic evaluation of summaries. In *Text summarization branches out*, pages 74–81.

Lopatina, O. L., Komleva, Y. K., Gorina, Y. V., Higashida, H., and Salmina, A. B. (2018). Neurobiological aspects of face recognition: The role of oxytocin. *Frontiers in Behavioral Neuroscience*, 12.

Lu, J., Xiong, C., Parikh, D., and Socher, R. (2017).

Knowing when to look: Adaptive attention via a visual sentinel for image captioning. In *Proceedings of the IEEE conference on computer vision and pattern recognition*, pages 375–383.

Ma, E. (2019). NLP Augmentation. https://github.com/makcedward/nlpaug.

Mafi, M., Martin, H., Cabrerizo, M., Andrian, J., Barreto, A., and Adjouadi, M. (2019). A comprehensive survey on impulse and gaussian denoising filters for digital images. *Signal Processing*, 157:236–260.

Mathews, A., Xie, L., and He, X. (2016). Senticap: Generating image descriptions with sentiments. In *Proceedings of the Thirtieth AAAI Conference on Artificial Intelligence*, AAAI'16, page 3574–3580. AAAI Press.

Mikolov, T., Chen, K., Corrado, G. S., and Dean, J. (2013). Efficient Estimation of Word Representations in Vector Space. In *ICLR*.

Mikolov, T., Grave, E., Bojanowski, P., Puhrsch, C., and Joulin, A. (2018). Advances in Pre-Training Distributed Word Representations. In *Proceedings of the Eleventh International Conference on Language Resources and Evaluation (LREC 2018)*, Miyazaki, Japan, May. European Language Resources Association (ELRA).

Nasir, O. R., Jha, S. K., Grover, M. S., Yu, Y., Kumar, A., and Shah, R. R. (2019). Text2facegan: Face generation from fine grained textual descriptions. In *2019 IEEE Fifth International Conference on Multimedia Big Data (BigMM)*, pages 58–67. IEEE.

Nezami, O. M., Dras, M., Wan, S., and Paris, C. (2020). Image captioning using facial expression and attention. *Journal of Artificial Intelligence Research*, 68:661–689.

Nie, W., Narodytska, N., and Patel, A. (2019). RelGAN: Relational generative adversarial networks for text generation. In *International Conference on Learning Representations*.

Niu, T. and Bansal, M. (2018). Adversarial oversensitivity and over-stability strategies for dialogue models. In *CoNLL*.

Panetta, K., Samani, A., Yuan, X., Wan, Q., Agaian, S. S., Rajeev, S., Kamath, S., Rajendran, R., Rao, S. P., Kaszowska, A., and Taylor, H. A. (2020). A Comprehensive Database for Benchmarking Imaging Systems. *IEEE Transactions on Pattern Analysis and Machine Intelligence*, 42:509–520.

Papineni, K., Roukos, S., Ward, T., and Zhu, W.-J. (2002). Bleu: a method for automatic evaluation of machine translation. In *Proceedings of the 40th annual meeting of the Association for Computational Linguistics*, pages 311–318.

Pedregosa, F., Varoquaux, G., Gramfort, A., Michel, V., Thirion, B., Grisel, O., Blondel, M., Prettenhofer, P., Weiss, R., Dubourg, V., Vanderplas, J., Passos, A., Cournapeau, D., Brucher, M., Perrot, M., and Duchesnay, E. (2011). Scikit-learn: Machine learning in Python. *Journal of Machine Learning Research*, 12:2825–2830.

Peng, C., Gao, X., Wang, N., Tao, D., Li, X., and Li, J. (2016). Multiple Representations-Based Face Sketch–Photo Synthesis. *IEEE Transactions on Neural Networks and Learning Systems*, 27:2201–2215.

Pennington, J., Socher, R., and Manning, C. D. (2014). GloVe: Global Vectors for Word Representation. In *EMNLP*.

Perov, I., Gao, D., Chervoniy, N., Liu, K., Marangonda, S., Umé, C., Dpfks, M., Facenheim, C. S., RP, L., Jiang, J., et al. (2020). Deepfacelab: A simple, flexible and extensible face swapping framework. *arXiv preprint arXiv: 2005.05535*.

Rumelhart, D. E., Hinton, G. E., and Williams, R. J., (1986). *Learning Internal Representations by Error Propagation*, page 318–362. MIT Press, Cambridge, MA, USA.

Sanh, V., Debut, L., Chaumond, J., and Wolf, T. (2019). DistilBERT, a distilled version of BERT: smaller, faster, cheaper and lighter. *ArXiv*, abs/1910.01108.

Sun, J., Li, Q., Wang, W., Zhao, J., and Sun, Z. (2021). Multi-caption text-to-face synthesis: Dataset and algorithm. In *Proceedings of the 29th ACM International Conference on Multimedia*, pages 2290–2298, New York, NY, USA. Association for Computing Machinery.

Wang, C., Yang, H., Bartz, C., and Meinel, C. (2016). Image captioning with deep bidirectional lstms. In *Proceedings of the 24th ACM international conference on Multimedia*, pages 988–997.

Wang, N., Gao, X., and Li, J. (2018). Random sampling for fast face sketch synthesis. *Pattern Recognit.*, 76:215–227.

Wang, Y., Pan, X., Song, S., Zhang, H., Huang, G., and Wu, C. (2019). Implicit semantic data augmentation for deep networks. *Advances in Neural Information Processing Systems*, 32.

Wang, Q., Meng, F., and Breckon, T. P. (2020). Data augmentation with norm-vae for unsupervised domain adaptation. *arXiv preprint arXiv:2012.00848*.

Xia, W., Yang, Y., Xue, J., and Wu, B. (2021). Tedigan: Text-Guided Diverse Face Image Generation and Manipulation. *2021 IEEE/CVF Conference on Computer Vision and Pattern Recognition (CVPR)*, pages 2256–2265.

Xie, Q., Dai, Z., Hovy, E., Luong, T., and Le, Q. (2020). Unsupervised data augmentation for consistency training. *Advances in Neural Information Processing Systems*, 33:6256–6268.

Xu, K., Ba, J., Kiros, R., Cho, K., Courville, A., Salakhudinov, R., Zemel, R., and Bengio, Y. (2015). Show, attend and tell: Neural image caption generation with visual attention. In *International conference on machine learning*, pages 2048–2057. PMLR.

Xu, T., Zhang, P., Huang, Q., Zhang, H., Gan, Z., Huang, X., and He, X. (2018). Attngan: Fine-grained text to image generation with attentional generative adversarial networks. In *Proceedings of the IEEE conference on computer vision and pattern recognition*, pages 1316–1324.

Yan, M., Zhao, M., Xu, Z., Zhang, Q., Wang, G., and Su, Z. (2019). Vargfacenet: An efficient variable group convolutional neural network for lightweight face recognition. In *Proceedings of the IEEE/CVF International Conference on Computer Vision Workshops*, pages 0–0.

Yang, Z., Dai, Z., Yang, Y., Carbonell, J. G., Salakhutdinov, R., and Le, Q. V. (2019). XLNet: Generalized Autoregressive Pretraining for Language Understanding. In *NeurIPS*.

Yu, J., Xu, X., Gao, F., Shi, S., Wang, M., Tao, D., and Huang, Q. (2020). Toward Realistic Face Photo-Sketch Synthesis via Composition-Aided GANs. *IEEE Transactions on Cybernetics*, PP:1–13, 03.

Zhang, Y., Ellyson, S., Zone, A., Gangam, P., Sullins, J., McCullough, C., Canavan, S., and Yin, L. (2011). Recognizing face sketches by a large number of human subjects: A perception-based study for facial distinctiveness. In *2011 IEEE International Conference on Automatic Face and Gesture Recognition and Workshops, FG 2011*, pages 707–712, 04.

Zhang, X., Zhao, J. J., and LeCun, Y. (2015). Character-level Convolutional Networks for Text Classification. *ArXiv*, abs/1509.01626.

Zhang, P., Li, X., Hu, X., Yang, J., Zhang, L., Wang, L., Choi, Y., and Gao, J. (2021). Vinvl: Making visual representations matter in vision-language models. *CVPR 2021*.

Zheng, Y., Yao, H., Sun, X., Zhang, S., Zhao, S., and Porikli, F. (2021). Sketch-specific data augmentation for freehand sketch recognition. *Neurocomputing*, 456:528–539.

Zhu, J.-Y., Park, T., Isola, P., and Efros, A. A. (2017). Unpaired image-to-image translation using cycle-consistent adversarial networks. In *Computer Vision (ICCV), 2017 IEEE International Conference on*.

Zhuang, L., Wayne, L., Ya, S., and Jun, Z. (2021). A Robustly Optimized BERT Pre-training Approach with Post-training. In *Proceedings of the 20th Chinese National Conference on Computational Linguistics*, pages 1218–1227, Huhhot, China, August. Chinese Information Processing Society of China.

10. Language Resource References

Hodosh, M., Young, P., and Hockenmaier, J. (2013). Framing Image Description as a Ranking Task: Data, Models and Evaluation Metrics (Extended Abstract). *J. Artif. Intell. Res.*, 47:853–899.

Tero Karras and Timo Aila and Samuli Laine and Jaakko Lehtinen. (2017). *Progressive Growing of GANs for Improved Quality, Stability, and Variation*.

Martinez, A. and Benavente, R. (1998). *The AR Face Database: CVC Technical Report, 24*. Department of Computer Science, Universitat Autònoma de Barcelona, January.

Phillips, P. Jonathon and Wechsler, Harry and Huang, Jeffrey and Rauss, Patrick J. (1998). *The FERET database and evaluation procedure for face-recognition algorithms*.

Wang, Xiaogang and Tang, Xiaoou. (2009a). *Face Photo-Sketch Synthesis and Recognition*.

Xiaogang Wang and Xiaoou Tang. (2009b). *Face Photo-Sketch Synthesis and Recognition*.

Zhang, W., Wang, X., and Tang, X. (2011). Coupled information-theoretic encoding for face photo-sketch recognition. In *CVPR 2011*, pages 513–520.

Appendix

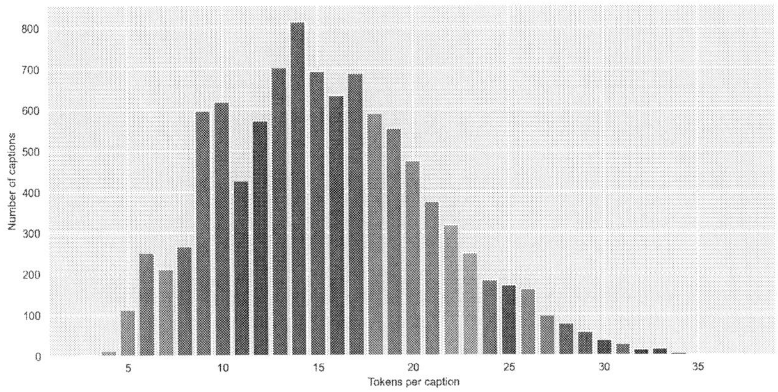

Figure 3: Distribution of captions based on their length in the CelebA-HQ dataset. The horizontal axis depicts token count per caption, the vertical axis represents caption count.

(a) Original caption: This man has double chin, bags under eyes, high cheekbones, mustache, big nose, goatee, and eyeglasses and wears hat. He is chubby. Feature annotations: Bags_Under_Eyes, Big_Lips, Big_Nose, Chubby, Double_Chin, Eyeglasses, Goatee, High_Cheekbones, Male, Mouth_Slightly_Open, Mustache, Smiling, Wearing_Hat.

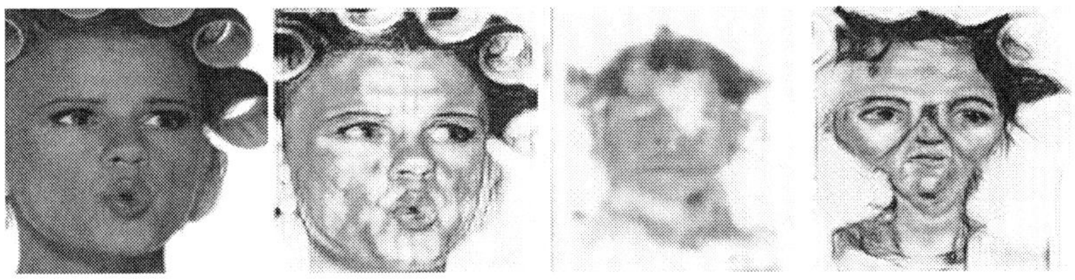

(b) Original caption: She is young and has mouth slightly open. Feature annotations: Mouth_Slightly_Open, No_Beard, Wearing_Necklace, Young

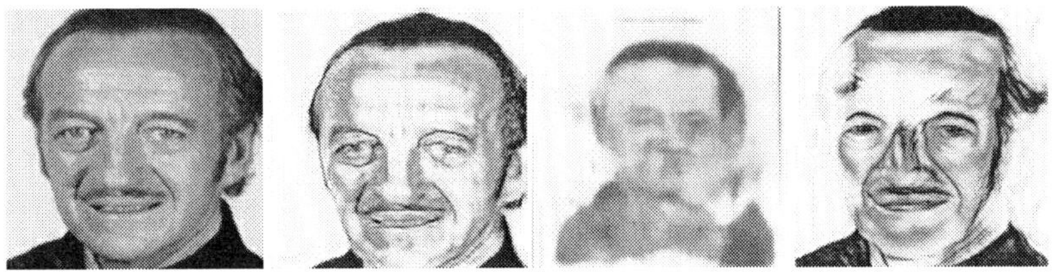

(c) Original caption: This person has mustache, big nose, and receding hairline. He is bald and wears necktie. He has beard.Feature annotations: Bags_Under_Eyes, Bald, Big_Nose, Chubby, Double_Chin, Male, Mouth_Slightly_Open, Mustache, Receding_Hairline, Smiling, Wearing_Necktie

Figure 4: Original picture in grey-scale versus the generated sketches. The images och each person display (from left to right): Original photo, Composite, Face2Sketch and Distorted models.

Original sentence:
This person is attractive, and young and has bags under eyes, wavy hair, arched eyebrows, and mouth slightly open.
word2vec:
substitution
This person is desirable, and spurn_materialism and has poly_bags ##under before_igniting_gunpowder, corkscrew_curls hair, arched eyebrows, and mouth minimally Pat_Barberot_Orchestra.
insertion
Massachusetts This person Mauer is UNH.N attractive, and young Indrajit and has Arun bags under eyes, Jack wavy Assa hair, arched eyebrows, and JUSTIN mouth slightly open.
GloVe:
substitution
This person is attractive, and both years has bags even eyes, wavy glasses, symmetrical eyebrows, taken tributary changed open.
insertion
This pask person aparece is attractive, and cnni young and has heberle bags under eyes, handson wavy friele hair, arched eyebrows, and mouth 102,500 slightly open.
fasttext:
substitution
Moreover person is attractive, and young and has bags beside eyes, wavy strawberry-blonde, bow-shaped question, thereafter mouth slowly locked.
insertion
Trinitresque This person LLU is attractive, and –Boston young and Finesilver has RoW bags under eyes, wavy Daksha hair, Jakar arched eyebrows, and Masturbator mouth slightly open.
BERT:
substitution
the man is attractive, and young and dark amber under eyes, wavy hair, arched eyebrows, but face tinted pink.
insertion
sometimes this person is attractive, short and so young and also has bags hiding under eyes, wavy silver hair, highly arched eyebrows, throat and mouth slightly open.
DistilBERT:
substitution
prehistoric lizard appeared attractive, appears young and has orange under thighs, red hair, arched ears, and mouth slightly open.
insertion
but this female person is attractive, and young and young has bags under blue eyes, wavy auburn hair, extremely arched eyebrows, and whose mouth slightly exposed open.
RoBERTA:
substitution
This female is attractive, and young and has bags under eyes, wavy hair, arched eyebrows, y mouth slightly open.
insertion
This person is attractive, fresh and also young and has bags under eyes, wavy hair, arched eyebrows, and mouth is slightly open.
WordNet (synonyms):
substitution
This person comprise attractive, and young and has bags under eyes, wavy hair, arched eyebrows, and mouth slightly open.
WordNet (antonyms):
substitution
This person differ repulsive, and old and lack bags under eyes, wavy hair, arched eyebrows, and mouth slightly unreceptive.
Manual (antonyms):
This person is not unattractive, and not old and doesn't have flat under eyes, straight hair, straight eyebrows, and mouth completely closed.

Table 2: Examples of caption augmentation with different methods available in the `nlpaug` tool. The image that these descriptions were produced for is the first image from Figure 4. For each model we show the results of both word-level substitution and insertion. Our best method is based on manual replacement of antonyms and is shown last.

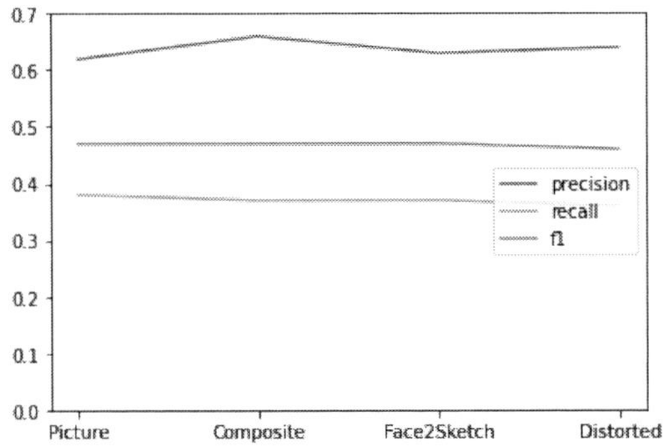

(a) Random Forest Micro

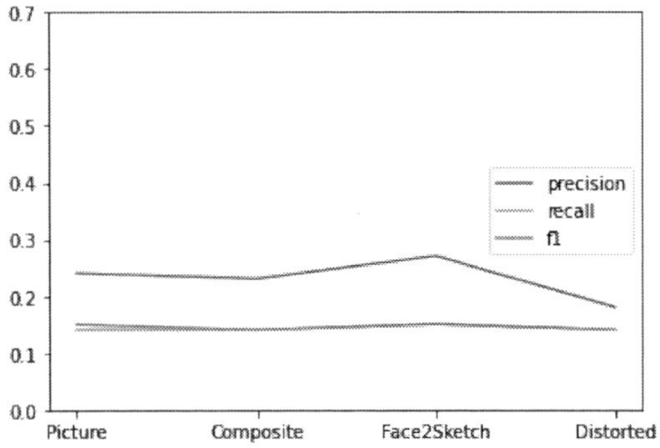

(b) Random Forest Macro

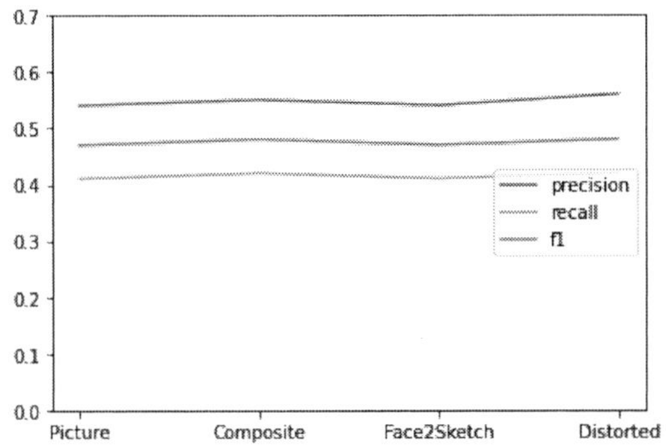

(c) k-NN Micro

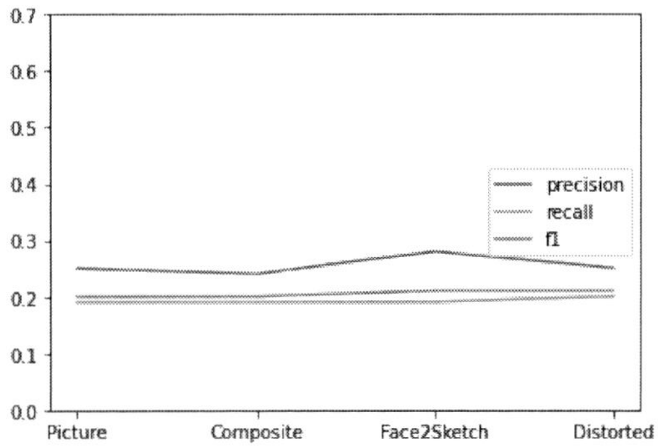

(d) k-NN Macro

Figure 5: Results of multi-label feature classification with different visual representations across multiple types of classifiers. The legend in each graph shows our evaluation metrics: precision, recall, F1-score. x axis corresponds to four different vision augmentation conditions, where **Picture** stands for original images. We set the maximum values on the y axis to 0.7 for visualisation purposes. We also report results for both Macro- and Micro-Averaged results per evaluation metric.

arched	straight
attractive	unattractive
bald	hairy
big	small
black	white
blond	dark
bushy	thin
chubby	skinny
double	single
grey	colourful
has	doesn't have
heavy	light
high	low
is	isn't
narrow	wide
no	any
open	closed
oval	square
pale	glowing
pointy	blunt
receding	widow's peak
rosy	pale
slightly	completely
smiling	frowning
straight	wavy
wavy	straight
wears	doesn't wear
young	old

Table 3: Each of the verbs, adjectives and adverbs found in original facial descriptions (left column) has been replaced with an antonym (right column) in our caption augmentation experiment. Note that some antonyms ("widow's peak") are much harder to ground into visual features.

Proceedings of the workshop on People in Vision, Language, and the Mind @LREC2022 , pages 41–47
Marseille, 20 June 2022
© European Language Resources Association (ELRA), licensed under CC-BY-NC-4.0

Face2Text revisited: Improved data set and baseline results

Marc Tanti[1], Shaun Abdilla[2], Adrian Muscat[3], Claudia Borg[4]
Reuben A. Farrugia[5], Albert Gatt[1,6]
[1]University of Malta, Institute of Linguistics and Language Technology
[2] [4] University of Malta, Department of Artificial Intelligence
[3] [5]University of Malta, Communications and Computer Engineering
[6]Utrecht University, Information and Computing Sciences
{marc.tanti, shaun.abdilla.07, adrian.muscat, claudia.borg, reuben.farrugia}@um.edu.mt, a.gatt@uu.nl

Abstract

Current image description generation models do not transfer well to the task of describing human faces. To encourage the development of more human-focused descriptions, we developed a new data set of facial descriptions based on the CelebA image data set. We describe the properties of this data set, and present results from a face description generator trained on it, which explores the feasibility of using transfer learning from VGGFace/ResNet CNNs. Comparisons are drawn through both automated metrics and human evaluation by 76 English-speaking participants. The descriptions generated by the VGGFace-LSTM + Attention model are closest to the ground truth according to human evaluation whilst the ResNet-LSTM + Attention model obtained the highest CIDEr and CIDEr-D results (1.252 and 0.686 respectively). Together, the new data set and these experimental results provide data and baselines for future work in this area.

Keywords: vision and language, image captioning, faces, language resources, natural language generation

1. Introduction

Image description generation models currently do not take into account the human element of facial description, and usually stop at either a very high-level (e.g. *A blonde woman*) or give incorrect facial descriptions (Nezami et al., 2018). A critical part of human-generated facial descriptions is a more in-depth analysis of the facial features themselves, sometimes including inferred emotions or expressions.

Developing data specifically focusing on facial description has benefits that go beyond the image description generation task. It would potentially improve information retrieval to the extent of making it easier for more accurate facial images to be obtained when searching the web, and more importantly, it would make software and web browsing a dramatically better experience for users with visual impairment (Makav and Kılıç, 2019). It is also helpful in forensic analysis (Jalan et al., 2020), bridging the gap between face descriptions and what those faces actually look like. This also affects the work being done in the inverse task of generating facial images from descriptions, which would lend the power of artificial intelligence to the work currently being done by (computer-aided) sketch artists. With enough data and a powerful enough model, the subjectivity that is currently intrinsic to sketching would be balanced out, ideally resulting in a generated face which is less biased and more likely to aid with the identification of people in the area of forensics. It would also be of benefit to the arts in the reverse task - books which describe a face can automatically generate depictions of what the character should look like, depending on the textual description. Casting of actors for a film adaptation could also be aided with a similar facial generation.

The objectives of the present work were (a) to encourage research in this direction with the development of a new data set of facial descriptions based on the CelebA data set of celebrity faces (Liu et al., 2015), and (b) to study the use of deep learning architectures (VGGFace/ResNet CNNs and LSTMs) for generating detailed descriptions from images of human faces. The models developed were evaluated by humans as well as using automatic metrics.

The rest of this paper is structured as follows. Section 2 provides a review of related data sets and models, mostly in the area of image description generation. Section 3 describes the development of the data set, whilst section 4 describes the baseline models. The models are evaluated and discussed in section 5, and section 6 concludes the paper.

2. Related work

2.1. Image description data sets

There is a wide variety of data sets for image description generation or image generation from descriptions. Some focus on scenes, such as MSCOCO (Lin et al., 2014) and WikiScenes (Wu et al., 2021), some on fine-grained object descriptions, such as Caltech-UCSD Birds and Oxford Flowers-102 (Reed et al., 2016), and others focus on multilingual descriptions, such as Multi30k (Elliott et al., 2016).

The original Face2Text data set (Gatt et al., 2018) – which the present work expands and improves upon – was the first data set to focus on faces. It was based on 400 photos from the Labelled Faces in the Wild data set (Huang et al., 2008) and the descriptions were collected through crowd sourcing. Prior to this data set, the closest to a facial description data set was CelebA (Liu et al., 2015) which is a collection of over 200k photos of celebrity faces obtained from the web, which pairs these images with data attributes such as hair colour and gender. This was followed by the Multi-Modal CelebA data set (Xia et al., 2021) which consists of 30 000 images from CelebA together with automatically constructed descriptions from the attributes. The limitation of this data set is that, since the descriptions are artificially constructed, they do not provide 'gold' annotations that give clues as to what people find salient in faces. Another facial description data set is FlickrFace11K (Nezami et al., 2018) which consists of 11 696 images extracted from Flickr30K (Young et al., 2014). Although the descriptions were written by humans, the images do not focus on the faces exclusively as they are scene photos and some photos contain more than one face. This made the descriptions lack the level of detail that we target in our data set.

Given the small size of the original Face2Text, the low quality face photos, and the low quality descriptions collected due to the nature of crowd sourcing, we revamped the data set to use CelebA images, and we sourced descriptions from human annotators who were hired for the purpose, and thoroughly briefed about the process.

2.2. Image description generation models

Image Description Generation models have the objective of generating global or dense descriptions for a given visual input, and hence require an understanding of both visual and linguistic elements. As in other areas of NLP, including vision and language processing, current image captioning models tend to be based on the pre-train-and-fine-tune paradigm, making use of Transformer-based architectures (Vaswani et al., 2017) pre-trained in a task-agnostic fashion on large (usually web-sourced) data sets (Sharma et al., 2018). Examples of such models include OSCAR (Li et al., 2020), VinVL (Zhang et al., 2021) and LEMON (Hu et al., 2021).

Since our goal in this paper is to establish baseline results, the remainder of this section focuses on classic attention-based encoder-decoder models, which are used in producing the baseline.

The Encoder-Decoder framework is arguably the standard model used in generating image descriptions. It works similarly to neural machine translation methods, with the image being the source and the sentence description being the target. In its most simple form, a Convolutional Neural Network (CNN) is used to encode the scene and the objects present in the image, together with their relationships. The output from the CNN is then passed into a sequence model, a Recurrent Neural Network (RNN) or derivatives of it, that acts as a conditioned language model which can be used to generate a sentence that is conditioned on the input image. For example, the Show and Tell image caption generator (Vinyals et al., 2014) uses a Long Short-Term Memory (LSTM) neural network to model the probability of a sentence given an input image.

Attention-based image description aims to generate suitable descriptions by paying attention only to the most visually relevant contents of an image, similarly to how primates and humans see and pay attention (Spratling and Johnson, 2004). The first work to use attention mechanisms in image description generation was the Show, Attend and Tell image caption generator (Xu et al., 2015), where an encoder-decoder model was fitted with an attention mechanism that would attend to salient parts of the image during the decoding process. Using an LSTM as a decoder, the attention mechanism selects visual features from the image and uses this to generate the next word in the sentence.

3. Data collection

At the time of publication, we have released two versions of the new Face2Text data set: version 1 and version 2. Both of these versions are publicly available[1]. The images are not included due to copyright reasons but can be downloaded separately from the CelebA data set (Liu et al., 2015). The baseline facial description generator was trained on version 1.

The annotation was done in two phases, for version 1 and 2. For version 1, 4 annotators were recruited and paid at a rate of €0.14 per caption. For version 2, 11 more annotators were recruited and paid at a rate of €0.08 per caption.

For each version, we selected a random sample of images from CelebA and stratified the sample such that the number of males and females depicted in the images was balanced. We then assigned a subset of the images to each annotator, depending on the number they were willing to annotate, such that no annotator annotated the same image more than once. The annotators then used a website, developed in-house, to write a description for each image. Annotators worked at their own pace and the data set was collected over the course of several months. Figure 1 shows a screenshot of the annotation tool.

The recruited annotators were students enrolled at the University of Malta. They first went through a trial run with 10 descriptions that were closely inspected before the annotators were engaged to do the entire allotment, thus ensuring quality. The instructions given to the annotators were the following:

- Describe the faces as naturally as possible.
- Do not spend too much time thinking about what to write. Just write the description which, in your view, accurately captures the physical attributes of the face.
- Don't describe the background and don't make inferences about the situation of the photo or the person (such as the person's job or background).

[1]Data sets can be downloaded from: `https://github.com/mtanti/face2text-dataset`.

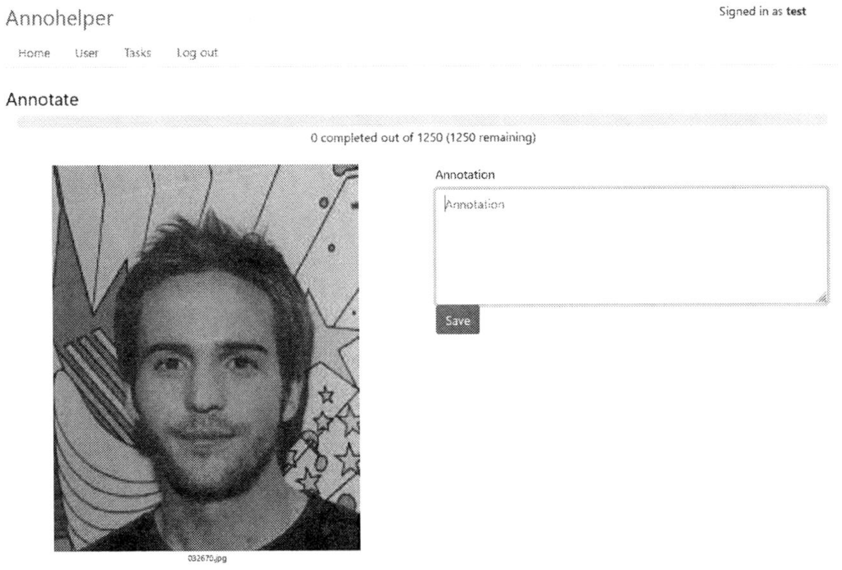

Figure 1: Screenshot of the annotation website developed for our annotators.

- You can describe a person's facial expression or their emotional state if this is evident from the picture.

- Given that the images are of celebrities, do not mention the names of people you recognise.

Furthermore, the annotators were made aware that their descriptions would be made public but that the annotators' identities would not be revealed. Prior to launching the study, we obtained clearance from the University of Malta Research Ethics Committee.[2]

3.1. Data statistics

Some examples of the descriptions obtained, together with a table of figures about the data sets are shown in Figure 2 and Table 1 respectively. Note that version 2 of the new data set is an extension of the data in version 1. None of the data from the original Face2Text data set was used in the new data sets.

	Orig.	v1	v2
Num. annotators	186	4	11
Num. images	400	4 076	10 559
Num. descriptions	1 445	5 685	17 022
Num. tokens	32 619	175 555	439 291
Num. token types	3 404	1 553	2 538
Descs./image	3.61	1.39	1.61
Descs./annotator	7.77	1 421.25	1 547.45
Tokens/description	22.57	30.88	25.81
Tokens/token type	9.58	113.04	173.09

Table 1: Quantitative summary of the Face2Text data sets. Note that 'Orig.' refers to the original Face2Text data set (Gatt et al., 2018) whilst 'v1' and 'v2' refer to version 1 and version 2 of the new data set described in this work.

4. Experiments

In this section we describe the baseline face description generator models we developed using version 1 of the new Face2Text data set. As already mentioned above, the models consist of an attention mechanism using a CNN as an encoder and an LSTM as a decoder. Variations are applied to this architecture to create different models and the results are reported.
The encoder CNN is either ResNet101 (He et al., 2015), which was pre-trained on the ImageNet data set (with the task of classifying the objects in an image), or VGG-Face (Schroff et al., 2015), which was pre-trained on the VGGFace data set (with the task of face recognition). These CNNs had their dense layers at the end removed to reveal the convolution layers and extract localised visual features from the images. They were also either fine-tuned or frozen during training.

The decoder LSTM either uses attention (Xu et al., 2015) or does not. The word embeddings are either taken from GloVe (Pennington et al., 2014) or are randomly initialised and fine-tuned with the rest of the model. Beam search is used to decode the sentences using beam sizes between 1 and 5.

For ease of reference, the model variants are denoted by 4-letter acronyms described in Table 2.

[2]https://www.um.edu.mt/research/ethics/

(a) *A woman with a chiselled jaw, prominent cheekbones, a long, narrow nose and thin eyebrows. She has long, messy, black hair and she is wearing makeup.*

(b) *A woman with long amber hair with black roots, having large cheeks and a small mouth, wearing makeup and red lipstick.*

(c) *A man with sun-tanned face, short brown hair, big downturned eyes and a wide smile.*

(d) *a white man with brown hair, open mouth and dark colored eyes*

Figure 2: Examples of descriptions in the data set.

Character	Meaning
R	ResNet encoder
V	VGG Face encoder
G	GloVe embeddings
E	No Pre-trained embeddings
F	Fine-tuned encoder
N	Encoder not fine-tuned
A	LSTM with attention decoder
L	LSTM decoder
1-5	Beam search size

Table 2: Character legend to the experiment variations.

5. Results

A number of evaluation metrics were applied to evaluate the performance of the face description generator. These were CIDEr, CIDEr-D, METEOR, and BLEU-1 to BLEU-5. Figure 3 shows a swarmplot of the top results.

The best performing model, according to CIDEr, was REFA, that is, fine-tuned ResNet CNN with randomly initialised word embeddings and attention. Further hyperparameter tuning was performed on the embedding size, LSTM size, and minibatch size of the top three variations (top three when the beam size is ignored) and the performance of the resulting models is shown in Table 3. REFA, the best model after tuning, has its hyperparameters listed in Table 4. Some example descriptions of the same image, from the best-performing models, are shown in Figure 4.

We also performed a human evaluation with 79 human evaluators. A random sample of 20 images was selected and each evaluator was asked to indicate on a 5-point Likert scale how fluent and correct (with respect to the image) each description was. Each image was accompanied by four descriptions: the generated descriptions from the top three models and the ground truth description. The highest median correctness score (equal to 4) was achieved by the RGFA descriptions (fine-tuned ResNet CNN with GloVe embeddings and attention), although these also have the highest variance. Fluency scores obtained by the RGFA were the most comparable to those obtained by the ground truth descriptions.

Model	METEOR	CIDEr	CIDEr-D
VEFA	45.83	1.078	0.581
RGFA	**47.80**	1.200	0.634
REFA	47.06	**1.212**	**0.662**

Table 3: Results of best three models after hyperparameter tuning using automatic evaluation.

Hyperparameter	Value
Optimiser	Adam
Learning rate	1×10^{-4}
Loss function	Cross entropy
Gradient clipping	5
Batch size	12
LSTM size	768
Embedding size	1024
Beam size	3

Table 4: Hyperparameter values of the best performing model: REFA.

6. Conclusions and future work

Our new Face2Text data set is a work-in-progress and we intend to continue adding more descriptions regularly, especially to balance the number of descriptions per image. The descriptions we have collected up to version 1 are good enough to make a strong baseline (if a pre-trained CNN is used).

We determined that, surprisingly, the ResNet CNN provides better features for a facial description generator

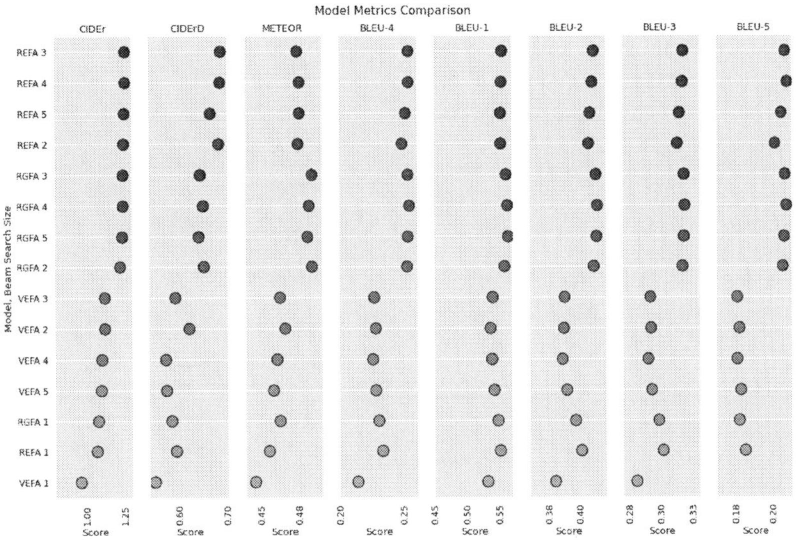

Figure 3: Swarmplot of evaluation metrics on the different variations of the face description generator.

Figure 4: Descriptions for the best described image:
Ground truth - *A young man with short brown hair and blue eyes. His lips are thin and his upper teeth are visible. He is smiling*
VEFA - *A man with short black hair thick eyebrows a wide nose and a smile with dimples*
RGFA/REFA - *A young man with short dark hair and small dark eyes. His lips are thin and his upper teeth are visible. He is smiling*

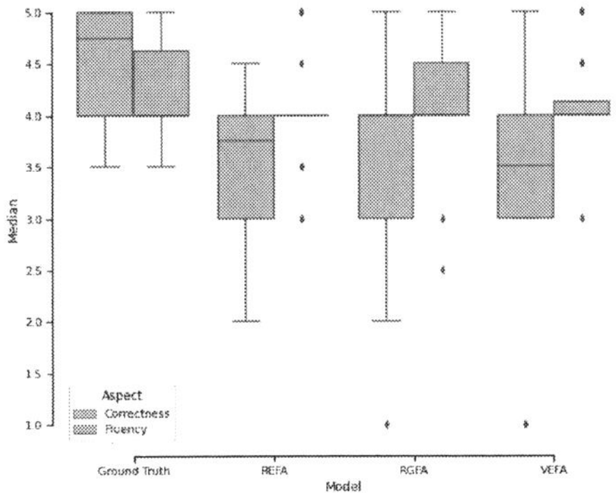

Figure 5: Results of best three models and ground truth using human evaluation.

than a face-specific CNN. Regardless of which CNN is used, it should always be fine-tuned. Whether to use pre-trained word embeddings or not does not seem to matter much but the use of attention is important. We also observe that on the face description task, one of our best performing baselines (REFA; cf Table 3) achieves CIDEr scores approaching those of comparable models (in the sense that they are encoder-decoder models based on recurrent units) in general scene description tasks such as MS-COCO. For example, the influential Top-Down Bottom-Up attention model with CIDEr optimisation achieves a score on MS-COCO of 1.201 (Anderson et al., 2018). Future work will however need to establish baselines on more recent, Transformer-based architectures.

In terms of further future work, the data set will benefit from more linguistic diversity, both in terms of writing style, as well as facial feature highlighting which would be useful for determining what is salient in a face.

7. Acknowledgements

This work was partly funded by the Malta Council for Science and Technology (MCST) - R&I-2019-004-T, and partly by a grant from the University of Malta Research Fund. The baseline model was developed as part of Shaun Abdilla's MSc project at the University of Malta.

8. Bibliographical References

Anderson, P., He, X., Buehler, C., Teney, D., Johnson, M., Gould, S., and Zhang, L. (2018). Bottom-up and top-down attention for image captioning and visual question answering. In *The IEEE Conference on Computer Vision and Pattern Recognition (CVPR)*, pages 6077–6086. IEEE Computer Society.

Elliott, D., Frank, S., Sima'an, K., and Specia, L. (2016). Multi30K: Multilingual English-German image descriptions. In *Proceedings of the 5th Workshop on Vision and Language*, pages 70–74, Berlin, Germany, August. Association for Computational Linguistics.

Gatt, A., Tanti, M., Muscat, A., Paggio, P., Farrugia, R. A., Borg, C., Camilleri, K. P., Rosner, M., and van der Plas, L. (2018). Face2Text: Collecting an annotated image description corpus for the generation of rich face descriptions. In *Proceedings of the Eleventh International Conference on Language Resources and Evaluation (LREC 2018)*, Miyazaki, Japan, May. European Language Resources Association (ELRA).

He, K., Zhang, X., Ren, S., and Sun, J. (2015). Deep residual learning for image recognition. *CoRR*, abs/1512.03385.

Hu, X., Gan, Z., Wang, J., Yang, Z., Liu, Z., Lu, Y., and Wang, L. (2021). Scaling Up Vision-Language Pre-training for Image Captioning. *ArXiv preprint 2111.12233*.

Huang, G. B., Mattar, M., Berg, T., and Learned-Miller, E. (2008). Labeled Faces in the Wild: A Database forStudying Face Recognition in Unconstrained Environments. In *Workshop on Faces in 'Real-Life' Images: Detection, Alignment, and Recognition*. Erik Learned-Miller and Andras Ferencz and Frédéric Jurie.

Jalan, H. J., Maurya, G., Corda, C., Dsouza, S., and Panchal, D. (2020). Suspect face generation. In *2020 3rd International Conference on Communication System, Computing and IT Applications (CSCITA)*, pages 73–78.

Li, X., Yin, X., Li, C., Zhang, P., Hu, X., Wang, L., Zhang, L., Hu, H., Dong, L., Wei, F., Choi, Y., and Gao, J. (2020). Oscar: Object-Semantics Aligned Pre-training for Vision-Language Tasks. In *Proceedings of the 16th European Conference on Computer Vision (ECCV'20)*, Glasgow, UK. Springer.

Lin, T.-Y., Maire, M., Belongie, S., Hays, J., Perona, P., Ramanan, D., Dollár, P., and Zitnick, C. L. (2014). Microsoft coco: Common objects in context. In David Fleet, et al., editors, *Computer Vision – ECCV 2014*, pages 740–755, Cham. Springer International Publishing.

Liu, Z., Luo, P., Wang, X., and Tang, X. (2015). Deep learning face attributes in the wild. In *Proceedings of International Conference on Computer Vision (ICCV)*.

Makav, B. and Kılıç, V. (2019). A new image captioning approach for visually impaired people. In *2019 11th International Conference on Electrical and Electronics Engineering (ELECO)*, pages 945–949.

Nezami, O. M., Dras, M., Anderson, P., and Hamey, L. (2018). Face-cap: Image captioning using facial expression analysis. *CoRR*, abs/1807.02250.

Pennington, J., Socher, R., and Manning, C. (2014). GloVe: Global vectors for word representation. In *Proceedings of the 2014 Conference on Empirical Methods in Natural Language Processing (EMNLP)*, pages 1532–1543, Doha, Qatar, October. Association for Computational Linguistics.

Reed, S., Akata, Z., Lee, H., and Schiele, B. (2016). Learning deep representations of fine-grained visual descriptions. In *2016 IEEE Conference on Computer Vision and Pattern Recognition (CVPR)*, pages 49–58.

Schroff, F., Kalenichenko, D., and Philbin, J. (2015). Facenet: A unified embedding for face recognition and clustering. In *2015 IEEE Conference on Computer Vision and Pattern Recognition (CVPR)*, pages 815–823.

Sharma, P., Ding, N., Goodman, S., and Soricut, R. (2018). Conceptual captions: A cleaned, hypernymed, image alt-text dataset for automatic image captioning. *Proceedings of the 56th Annual Meeting of the Association for Computational Linguistics (ACL'18)*, pages 2556–2565.

Spratling, M. W. and Johnson, M. H. (2004). A feedback model of visual attention. *J. Cognitive Neuroscience*, 16(2):219–237.

Vaswani, A., Shazeer, N., Parmar, N., Uszkoreit, J., Jones, L., Gomez, A. N., and Kaiser, Ł. (2017). Attention Is All You Need. In *Proceedings of the 31st Conference on Neural Informaton Processing Systems (NeurIPS'17)*, Long Beach, CA.

Vinyals, O., Toshev, A., Bengio, S., and Erhan, D. (2014). Show and tell: A neural image caption generator. *CoRR*, abs/1411.4555.

Wu, X., Averbuch-Elor, H., Sun, J., and Snavely, N. (2021). Towers of babel: Combining images, language, and 3d geometry for learning multimodal vision. In *Proceedings of the IEEE/CVF International Conference on Computer Vision (ICCV)*, pages 428–437, October.

Xia, W., Yang, Y., Xue, J.-H., and Wu, B. (2021). Tedigan: Text-guided diverse face image generation and manipulation. In *IEEE Conference on Computer Vision and Pattern Recognition (CVPR)*.

Xu, K., Ba, J., Kiros, R., Cho, K., Courville, A. C., Salakhutdinov, R., Zemel, R. S., and Bengio, Y. (2015). Show, attend and tell: Neural image caption generation with visual attention. *CoRR*, abs/1502.03044.

Young, P., Lai, A., Hodosh, M., and Hockenmaier, J. (2014). From image descriptions to visual denotations: New similarity metrics for semantic inference over event descriptions. *Transactions of the Association for Computational Linguistics*, 2:67–78.

Zhang, P., Li, X., Hu, X., Yang, J., Zhang, L., Wang, L., Choi, Y., and Gao, J. (2021). VinVL: Revisiting Visual Representations in Vision-Language Models. In *Proceedings of the IEEE Computer Society Conference on Computer Vision and Pattern Recognition (CVPR'21)*, pages 5575–5584.

Author Index